CELEBRATING EXCELLENCE
THE DESTINY OF BLACK WOMEN IN AMERICA

Tolbert Morris

Copyright © 2024 Tolbert Morris

All rights reserved.

No part of this publication may be reproduced, distributed, or transmitted in any form or by any means, including photocopying, recording, or other electronic or mechanical methods, without the prior written permission of the publisher, except in the case of brief quotations embodied in critical reviews and certain other noncommercial uses permitted by copyright law.

To my beloved mother, Janie Howard

You are the guiding star that has illuminated my path through life. Your nurturing care and boundless love have shaped me into the person I am today. I am forever grateful for your unwavering support, for you are the cornerstone of my existence. You taught me that caring for others is not just an obligation but a calling. Their pain became my own, and their burdens were not a weight but an opportunity for me to shine as a beacon of hope. Your selfless devotion to those in need has inspired me to follow in your compassionate footsteps.

I carry with me the invaluable lessons and wisdom imparted not only by you, but also by the incredible women who have graced my existence. To my loving wife, Janice Morris, whose support and understanding have been a constant source of strength and encouragement. To Olivia Howard, my dear sister, whose kindness and generosity have taught me the true meaning of empathy. To Delores Daniels, whose strength and resilience have been a testament to the power of the human spirit. To Hattie Crenshaw, my sister, whose wisdom and guidance have been a source of unwavering support. And to Annie Kate Stockton, my sister, whose unwavering belief in the potential of humanity has shown me the importance of faith.

We of African American descent are indebted to the remarkable women who have paved the way for progress, justice, and equality. Women like Harriet Tubman, who fearlessly led enslaved individuals to freedom on the Underground Railroad. Women like Rosa Parks, who sparked the Montgomery Bus Boycott and played a pivotal role in the civil rights movement. Women like Maya Angelou, whose words and wisdom continue to inspire and empower. Women like Shirley Chisholm, who broke barriers as the first Black woman elected to the U.S. Congress.

Today, African American women continue to shape the present and future of our community and our nation. Women like Kamala Harris, who made history as the first female, Black, and Asian Vice President of the United States. Women like Ava DuVernay, who uses her filmmaking prowess to tell stories that challenge and inspire. Women like Stacey Abrams, who tirelessly advocates for voting rights and civic engagement.

This book is a small token of my gratitude to these extraordinary women who have enriched the lives of all Americans with their love and wisdom. They are a testament to the resilience and strength of African American women throughout history, and they continue to light the way for a brighter future.

With all my love and deepest appreciation,

Tolbert Morris

Table of Contents

Chapter ONE

Introduction ... 1
   1.1 Significance of Black Women's Contributions ... 1
   1.2 Historical Context ... 2

Chapter TWO

The Struggle for Equality ... 4
   2.1 African American Women's Role in the Civil Rights Movement ... 4
   2.2 Challenges Faced by Black Women Throughout History ... 6
   2.3 Intersectionality of Race and Gender ... 9

Chapter THREE

Breaking Barriers in Education and Academia ... 11
   3.1 Pioneering Black Women in Education ... 11
   3.2 African American Women's Impact on Higher Education ... 14
   3.3 Overcoming Obstacles in Pursuit of Education ... 18

Chapter FOUR

The Power of Black Women in Arts and Culture ... 21
   4.1 Influential Black Female Artists ... 21
   4.2 Black Women in Literature and Poetry ... 24
   4.3 Celebrating Black Women in Film and Television ... 28

Chapter FIVE

Business and Entrepreneurship ... 37
   5.1 Black Women Trailblazers in Business ... 37
   5.2 Challenges and Triumphs in Corporate America ... 41
   5.3 Empowering the Next Generation of Black Women Entrepreneurs ... 44

Chapter SIX

Politics and Activism 47
   6.1 Notable Black Women in Politics 47
   6.2 Black Women's Impact in Grassroots Movements 58
   6.3 Advocacy for Social Justice and Policy Change 63

Chapter SEVEN

Health and Wellness 69
   7.1 Black Women and Healthcare Disparities 69
   7.2 Promoting Health and Wellness in Black Communities 74
   7.3 Addressing Mental Health in Black Women 77

Chapter EIGHT

Role Models and Inspirational Figures 80
   8.1 Icons and Trailblazers 80
   8.2 Unsung Heroes and Local Legends 90
   8.3 Inspiring Stories of Resilience and Achievement 93

Chapter NINE

Future Prospects and Challenges 101
   9.1 Building on Successes and Momentum 101
   9.2 Continuing to Address Intersectionality 105
   9.3 Embracing Empowerment and Equality for All 110

Conclusion

   Reflecting on Black Women's Contributions 117
   Looking Towards a Brighter Future 119

Preface

Welcome to "Celebrating Excellence: The Destiny of Black Women in America." In these pages, we embark on an enlightening journey that explores the remarkable and influential contributions of Black women throughout history. This captivating book acknowledges the indispensable role these women have played in shaping the nation, highlighting their resilience, fortitude, and unwavering spirit.

It is imperative to recognize and celebrate the achievements of Black women, for their impact is profound and far-reaching. By shedding light on their stories, we honor the legacy of our grandmothers, mothers, sisters, and all women who have paved the way for future generations. This celebration is not intended to minimize the struggles and accomplishments of Black men; rather, it seeks to emphasize the importance of recognizing and honoring the unique successes of Black women.

Understanding the historical context, we must also acknowledge the distressing trend of appropriating the work, ideas, and creative genius of Black women without proper credit or citation. These acts of appropriation have perpetuated a cycle of erasure and marginalization. With the advent of the internet, this issue has become even more prominent.

To combat these acts of appropriation, it is crucial that Black women are properly credited and cited for their work and ideas. By acknowledging and celebrating their contributions, we honor their achievements while actively working towards a more inclusive and accurate historical narrative. Individuals and institutions must engage in efforts that amplify the voices and experiences of Black women, actively supporting their visibility and fostering a fair and just society.

In "The Destiny of Black Women in America," we rejoice in the accomplishments of Black women who have shaped and continue to shape the nation. This book celebrates their triumphs and highlights their destined path to becoming leaders in America. By delving into their stories, we gain a deeper understanding of the united front that has propelled both genders toward greater heights of achievement and equality.

Come, join us on this journey of discovery and admiration as we celebrate the indelible mark Black women have left on American history. Let us recognize, honor, and learn from their extraordinary accomplishments, forging a brighter future in which their contributions are rightly acknowledged and celebrated.

Chapter **One**

Introduction

1.1 Significance of Black Women's Contributions

Welcome to Celebrating Excellence: The Destiny of Black Women in America. As you hold this book in your hands, I want to explicitly state that I use the term "Black" instead of "African American" to acknowledge the historical context of our People's journey. Our history began in America when slaves were not recognized as citizens, but rather as property—dehumanized and stripped of basic human rights. It was in the 1970s that being Black became a symbol of pride and self-awareness, with James Brown famously declaring, "Say it loud, I'm black, and I'm proud." This choice is not meant as an insult to those who prefer "African American", but rather as a simple affirmation of pride and recognition for those who lived their lives as Black individuals.

This book, Celebrating Excellence: The Destiny of Black Women in America, offers an honest exploration of what it truly means to be a Black woman in the United States. Throughout centuries, imperialist powers worldwide waged a war against the Black community. This war not only invaded their land but also subjected

Black individuals to inhumane treatment, perpetuating a superiority complex among those in power. It is astonishing to think that just a few centuries ago, Black people were treated as commodities, traded as if their lives held no value. The harsh reality is that some people have experienced the world's cruelty firsthand, and we must face this bitter truth.

But this book isn't solely focused on reopening old wounds. Instead, it serves as an acknowledgment of the resilience and resistance displayed by Black women. They ensured that future generations would not bear the same horrors they endured and fearlessly fought against oppression. It serves as a reminder to people worldwide of the courageous acts performed by Black women which should forever be taught in schools across the globe.

Often, discussions about the impact of slavery and its aftermath fail to recognize the role of Black women. While male abolitionists have been discussed extensively, the contribution of women in the fight against slavery often goes unmentioned. This book seeks to provide a different perspective, moving beyond the traditional narratives and offering a lens focused on the experiences, perspectives, and remarkable accomplishments of Black women. Nevertheless, in celebrating Black women, this book does not belittle the efforts of Black men in the ongoing struggle for equality and justice. It highlights the bond between Black men and women and their unity in fighting against the formidable forces of their time.

1.2 Historical Context

The journey within this book commences with a historical account of slavery in the United States and the torment endured by Black people during this dark period in human history. As readers become acquainted with the horrors of the past, they will be shocked at how power can blind even the most empathetic individuals. Moreover, as you learn about the resilience displayed by Black women and men, you will be reassured that there is always hope amidst adversity. The achievements of the Black community are nothing short of incredible, and their determination shines through in recent fights against inequality, where they boldly advocate for their rights while raising their voices for marginalized communities and nations worldwide.

Celebrating Excellence: The Destiny of Black Women in America also aims to encourage individuals to take full responsibility for their lives and live with purpose. Nothing is greater than fighting for oneself, and nothing is more worthy of respect than a life lived with dignity. Therefore, we pay tribute to the countless Black women and men who have redefined perseverance and determination, they have shown the world that relinquishing control of one's destiny is never the answer and that rising above adversity is the only way forward.

Within the pages of this book, we honor the heroes who have departed and those who continue to walk among us. We remain dedicated to following in their footsteps and incorporating the valuable lessons they instilled in us years ago. In paying our respects, we acknowledge the incredible courage it takes to swim against the tide when the currents are strong and pulling you in the opposite direction.

Welcome to Celebrating Excellence: The Destiny of Black Women in America—a testament to the triumphs, struggles, and indomitable spirit of Black women throughout history. May it illuminate the path toward equality, justice, and a future where every individual is empowered to embrace their destiny.

Chapter Two

The Struggle for Equality

2.1 African American Women's Role in the Civil Rights Movement

It is important for us to acknowledge the brutal reality of slavery and the suffering endured by enslaved Black women. They were not only deprived of their freedom but also subjected to various forms of exploitation and abuse. Many were forced to work long hours in labor fields or in the homes of their masters, facing physical and emotional hardships daily. Tragically, sexual exploitation was also a harsh reality for many of these women, who had no choice but to silently endure the demands of their masters.

The separation from their families added another layer of pain, as Black girls were often torn away from their parents at a young age and made to live with their owners. Despite these unimaginable circumstances, it is awe-inspiring to learn about the remarkable courage and resilience that some women displayed in breaking free from the chains of slavery.

Celebrating Excellence

However, it is crucial that we not overlook the suffering that these women experienced. By taking the time to understand and uncover the dehumanizing aspects of slavery, we show respect for all those who fought for a better future. It's through this understanding that we can contribute to ensuring that future generations do not have to endure the complexities of the past, nor be subjected to discrimination, inequality, or low-paying jobs.

For decades, enslaved Black people were deprived of dignity and respect, and there was hardly anyone who extended a helping hand to them. Slave owners would get involved in human trade, snatching people away and bringing them with them to their lands, mines, homes, etc.—to exploit them and make them work without pay, and while it is indeed remarkable to witness the courage of women who broke away from the shackles of slavery, it is important to pause and reflect on their suffering. Instead of glossing over the hard time they had, it is quite vital (as a form of respect for all those who struggled to ensure that their future generations will not suffer the intricacies of the past or bow down to anyone) to not forget the dehumanizing aspects of slavery and the impacts the cruel system had on Black women.

Not only were those women made to work in labor fields or at the homes of their master's for hours, but they had no other choice but to silently accept the "other demands" of their masters. At a place, far away from their homes, enslaved Black women suffered silently, and secretly prayed for a life where they could be free and nurture their own children. The abuse didn't end there. Many Black women were sexually exploited so that they could bear children, which ensured an increase in the number of slaves for the future without any additional cost. If women got pregnant 'accidentally', many underwent complicated and unsafe abortion procedures to end the pregnancy. Things were not easy for Black women who entered motherhood, many Black women chose to live as bonded labor for the sake of their children, as it ensured that they would be close to nurturing their own children. Running away from the toxicity was not an option. First, these women were far away from their homes and had no means to go back to where they came from. Second, they had no financial independence. Slaves were forced to perform unpaid labor for their wealthy masters.

Over the years, the systemic oppression and the lack of opportunities became suffocating. Anger and frustration kept building up, and the enslaved population rose against their oppressors. It was at this moment when a Black woman, Harriet Tubman, became the symbol of resistance and the abolitionist movement.

2.2 Challenges Faced by Black Women Throughout History

"In my mind, I see a line. And over that line, I see green fields and lovely flowers and beautiful white women with their arms stretched out to me over that line, but I can't seem to get there no-how. I can't seem to get over that line." This quote is attributed to Harriet Tubman, a fierce conductor of The Underground Railroad.

Harriet Tubman should be a role model for every person who needs some motivation to do things they know they can achieve but seem to be paralyzed because of the fear of the unknown. Harriet Tubman was a slave, and yet she played a big role in freeing hundreds of slaves, bringing them from one part of the U.S. to another and helping them find a job for themselves.

There's another quote by Harriet Tubman that explains what it feels like to finally cross the "line". This is what she said: "When I found

Celebrating Excellence

I had crossed that line, I looked at my hands to see if I was the same person. There was such glory over everything; the sun came like gold through trees, and over the fields, and I felt like I was in Heaven."

There is always a light at the end of the tunnel; all that a person is required to do is to keep moving and looking forward. It doesn't matter where you are or what you're going through, if you have the passion or drive to change your life, or circumstances, you can do so. While the struggle may seem a little difficult, victory is all yours.

Take Harriet Tubman's example for a second. This strong woman was born into slavery, and throughout her life, she remained neglected and deprived of liberty. But she didn't accept her fate and struggled for her happiness. She once said, "I grew up like a neglected weed—ignorant of liberty, having no experience of it. Then I was not happy or content…"

She didn't let fate decide what came next for her and took charge of her life. She wasn't happy with what she had, so she struggled to change it. There were many times when Harriet stood up for herself. That was the time when the U.S. was still dominated by slave owners who didn't like Harriet's rebellious nature. As she kept freeing slaves, anger among slave owners grew. And when it passed the tolerance threshold, they announced reward money for anyone who would help catch Harriet (dead or alive).

It truly is remarkable how Harriet Tubman defied the odds and achieved so much despite the adversities she faced. From being a neglected slave, she rose to become known as the "Moses of her people" and even received military honors at her funeral. It's noteworthy that she is set to become the first Black person to appear on the U.S. dollar bill, replacing former President Andrew Jackson on the $20 bill by 2030.

Who could have imagined that a woman who once endured the life of a slave, witnessing only the harsh realities of slavery, would ultimately rise to become the most revered figure in America's financial system, an eminent force on the global stage? Slave owners who tried to punish her for her actions could not have known that years later, the U.S. would have statues and parks named after her. This is Black Excellence, and this is what people should strive for. Harriet Tubman's life shows that you can achieve your goals even when everything in this world is set against you.

It is easy to feel motivated and determined when everything is going in your favor. It is easy to feel good when you know that you can easily navigate through the system. But it is difficult when you must deal with a system that is inherently against you. And that's when you have real growth. Harriet Tubman's legacy as a role model spans generations even after her passing, as she exemplified the power of taking control of one's life and pursuing ambitions with unwavering determination. If you ever find yourself in life-altering situations, let the same fiery passion that this courageous woman possessed guide you towards discovering your own path.

To no fault of their own, Black women were living in a world where supremacists enjoyed power. It was not their fault that most "civilized" nations gave a green signal to the slave trade. But instead of waiting for the lady luck to knock on their door, they knocked first, stood up, and carved their fate.

2.3 Intersectionality of Race and Gender

When Barrack Obama became president, it was an indescribable moment for hundreds of thousands of people. The moment showed that the system was inclusive and open to the Black community. When young Black men looked at Barrack Obama, many of them believed it was possible for them to become president as well. They developed the passion to enter the country's political arena.

Compare this to the time when Black people lived as an enslaved population. This clearly shows that people can achieve the impossible if they have the drive to keep moving and keep fighting. Nothing is impossible for you! It is also important to accept who you are and use your strengths to achieve your goals. Now, take a moment and try to recall the 2008 moment. Imagine a child watching the ceremony and realizing that all the goals that they had marked as impossible were beginning to look a lot easier to accomplish.

When you imagine yourself involved in a movement that fights for the civil rights of a particular race, it brings forth a sense of conviction and determination. With such passion and determination, achieving the dream of equality and justice for that race becomes very much attainable. History has shown us that dedicated individuals and communities can bring about significant social change. By joining forces, raising awareness, and fighting for justice, we can make a tangible difference and create a more inclusive society. It may take time and effort, but with belief and unwavering determination, the dream of achieving civil rights for all people is achievable.

This is why it's important to celebrate Black Women's Excellence. It gives you a reason to believe that your aspirations are worth fighting for. Today, when Black girls and women read about Harriet Tubman or Rosa Parks, they develop an urge to be like them. They see themselves in them and resolve to have what they have—determination, courage, wit, and nerves of steel.

These heroes still teach young kids that while the system can be against them—while they may be asked to abandon their dreams—they must keep their heads high and move forward. They must find a purpose in their life and work for it; they must remind themselves that they can shatter the barriers set on their way to success and progress.

Chapter Three

Breaking Barriers in Education and Academia

3.1 Pioneering Black Women in Education

For Black women, the struggle against racism, inequality, and segregation came at a very young age. Ruby Bridges was six when she became the center of attention. Her story also provides a unique perspective to everyone looking for some guidance to move ahead.

In the wake of the 1954 Supreme Court verdict held in the Brown vs. The Board of Education, case where all schools were ordered to segregate, Ruby Bridges was selected to take a test that would determine whether she was eligible to attend an all-white school. Ruby Bridges passed the test.

Prior to this though, Ruby Bridges also had to travel miles every day to attend an all-black school, although she lived only a few blocks away from an all-white elementary school. Such was the tyranny of school segregation, forcing children to put their comfort aside and make long, arduous journeys every day if they wanted to attend school.

As she passed the test, she was admitted to an all-white school, becoming the first Black child to attend such a school. This did not sit well in a society where racism and aversion to Black people were deeply ingrained, and Ruby Bridges—at the tender age of six—became the face of resilience and steadfastness.

Her presence at the school pricked the fragile ego of white supremacists who strongly objected to the Supreme Court ruling. For Ruby Bridges, every day was a struggle. She faced racism at school and from parents of other children who were appalled at the idea of having their children attend school with a Black child. Many parents pulled their children out of school in protest. The situation turned so bad that federal marshals had to escort Ruby Bridges and her mother to the school. This was so done because people outside her school would throw things at her to record their anger over the court's decision to desegregate. One woman crossed all the limits and brought a black doll in a wooden coffin.

Inside the school, the situation was not perfect either. Teachers refused to teach the little girl, who eventually found the accepting arms of Ms. Barbara Henry—the sole teacher who agreed to teach her. Ruby Bridges remained her only student as most parents pulled out their children and refused to let them sit with a Black girl. This went on for at least a year, but by the second year, things started to get better. She was no longer escorted by federal marshals, and she attended classes with other students.

At such a young age, no child should go through what Ruby Bridges went through. But had she backed away or lost her spirit, hundreds of thousands of Black students who now find a safe learning environment at schools would not have found a way to get ahead in life. The anger that she was met with can break anyone, after all, no one likes being told that they are not welcome at a particular place.

It's truly heartbreaking to imagine how a small child like Ruby Bridges must have felt when confronted with such discrimination and hostility from other children and their parents. Experiencing such rejection and racism at such a young age could easily discourage anyone and hinder the pursuit of their dreams. Ruby Bridges could have easily had second thoughts about attending the all-white school, even with the knowledge that her admission wasn't merely a result of pity or charity. However, she knew that she had rightfully earned her place by passing a test and demonstrating her capabilities. Despite the distance and the challenges she faced, Ruby Bridges persevered and showed immense courage in pursuing her education. Her story is a powerful testament to her strength and determination.

In our lives, unexpected circumstances can often lead us down completely different paths, making it difficult to predict what lies ahead. When faced with a series of obstacles, it's natural to question ourselves and our abilities. Interestingly, the real struggle sometimes begins after we achieve the goals we set for ourselves. This was certainly the case for Ruby Bridges. Receiving admission to an all-white school was a significant milestone for her, but it was just the beginning of her journey. The hardships she endured shaped her into an iconic figure who dedicated herself tirelessly to promoting tolerance in society. Had she not faced those challenges, she might not have become the influential advocate she is today.

3.2 African American Women's Impact on Higher Education

What is the best way for all people to get ahead in their lives? It is to get an education—to have a degree that can open the doors for them. Today, we see many Black women at top universities. We saw Black women in the arts, in tech, in finance, and in almost all other fields. But times were not always on the side of Black women—in fact, for a majority of Black people, during Jim Crow and the Civil Rights movement, having a decent paying job was the ultimate goal; a high school education was rare for many, and having a college education was unthinkable for most.

Today, it is one of the most important things a person can do for themselves. For an individual to be educated would mean that they have sacrificed both time and money on their career and are deserving of the "American Dream." In the years after slavery and the beginning of the 20th century, however, an education above high school was not as important.

For women especially, an education was incredibly rare. Even more unheard of was a Black woman with a college degree. A Black woman's goal of pursuing a college degree was made exceedingly difficult because no college was interested in admitting (or willing to admit) a Black woman onto a college campus unless she was there for domestic purposes.

But there was some resistance. And we had Black educators who changed history. More than ever, it is so important to highlight the achievements of Black educators in the teaching profession. Not only is it crucial to give them long-overdue recognition, but it also helps to remind us of how far the educational system has come and how far we have left to go. As educators, we should be at the forefront of acknowledging how much the Black community has endured being an active part of the American education system.

Here are some Black educators who made a significant impact on history (this information was researched and imposed by information first written by Jamie O'Killian):

Mary McLeod Bethune

Mary McLeod Bethune became one of the most important civil rights leaders of the 20th century. She was a lifelong educator—working as a teacher before founding Bethune-Cookman College which sets educational standards for today's Black colleges. She went on to become the highest-ranking Black woman in government when President Franklin Roosevelt named her director of Negro Affairs of the National Youth Administration.

Fannie Jackson Coppin

Fanny Jackson Coppin was the first Black principal. Born as a slave, she once wrote to Frederick Douglas, "I feel sometimes like a person to whom in childhood was entrusted some sacred flame…This is the desire to see my race lifted out of the mire of ignorance, weakness, and degradation; no longer to sit in obscure corners and devour the scraps of knowledge which his superiors flung at him. I want to see him crowned with strength and dignity; adorned with the enduring grace of intellectual attainments."

Inez Beverly Prosser

Inez Beverly Prosser, the first Black woman to earn a Ph.D. in Psychology, Inez Beverly Prosser did extensive research on the effect of segregated schools versus non-segregated schools on Black students. She was passionate about finding the best way to foster and educate young black students. She was also one of the first to take a vested interest in the mental health of Black children subjected to racism.

Dr. Jeanne L. Noble

Dr. Jeanne L. Noble, a professor of education, was active in trying to desegregate her hometown of Augusta, GA. She was appointed by three presidents (Johnson, Nixon, and Ford) to serve on educational commissions.

Septima Poinsette Clark

Septima Poinsette Clark was an educator and civil rights activist. Clark developed the literacy and citizenship workshops that played an important role in the drive for voting rights and civil rights for Blacks in the Civil Rights Movement. Septima Clark's work was commonly under-appreciated by Southern male activists. Martin Luther King Jr. commonly referred to Septima P. Clark as the "Mother" of the Civil Rights Movement in the United States.

A recent study in 2018 examines the expectations and stereotypes that Black women face at colleges and universities in the United States. The study—co-authored by Bridget Turner Kelly, a University of Maryland associate professor—identifies a need for diverse support structures for Black women at educational institutions, particularly at predominantly white institutions (PWIs). "Black women have historically been marginalized both for their race and gender, which led us to look at the intersectionality of race and gender at predominantly white institutions," Dr. Kelly says. "Building upon the foundations laid by their predecessors, we study the role of education as the gateway to leadership positions for Black women in America. We explore institutions and initiatives dedicated to empowering and uplifting Black women, such as Historically Black Colleges and Universities (HBCUs)."

Over the past decade-plus, Black women have been overachieving in the classrooms, according to a report by the National Center for Education Statistics that was released in 2020, the most recent year the data was made available.

More good news is on the horizon as U.S. employers expect to hire 31.6 percent more Black college graduates this year, which means there will be a wealth of opportunities for those coming out of school looking to find work in today's tough market, but students will need to stand out and acquire a multitude of skills to stay competitive. Studies show that Black women are doing just that.

According to the National Center for Education Statistics (NCES), between 2018 and 2019, Black women made up 68 percent of associate degrees, 66 percent of bachelor's degrees, 71 percent of Master's degrees, and 65 percent of doctoral, medical, and dental degrees.

The numbers are lower for Black women venturing into the world of computer science and STEM. (Science, technology, engineering, and mathematics). The group only represents 4.2 percent of biology sciences, 2.6 percent of computer sciences, 2.8 percent of physical sciences, and 2.3 percent of math and statistics degrees, the National Center for Science and Engineering notes.

While education may be soaring to new heights for Black women across the United States, pay disparities continue to haunt the community and even those with the most impressive qualifications. On average, Black women earn 38 percent less than white men every year. Black women are more likely to be employed in sectors such as health care, education, and hospitality, all of which often pay lower in terms of wages. Even those who are working in high-paying fields, such as physicians and surgeons, still feel the unfortunate burn of pay inequality, making 54 cents for every dollar paid to their white, non-Hispanic male counterparts. Despite having some of the highest labor force rates, overall, Black women earn just 64 cents for every dollar earned by white, non-Hispanic men in 2020.

Overall, while Black women are certainly obtaining more degrees, there is more work to be done to ensure they can make a fair living post-graduation. The data may be gloomy, but the news does show a promising sign that Black women are working diligently to close the wealth gap and build brighter futures for themselves and their families. Some are becoming the first in their family to attend college, beating the immense odds.

3.3 Overcoming Obstacles in Pursuit of Education

Many Black female organizations exist today to address the unique experiences, challenges, and needs of Black women. They strive to create spaces where Black women can come together to support and empower each other, advocate for their rights, and drive positive change in their communities. These organizations often focus on a range of issues, such as intersectional feminism, racial justice, educational and economic opportunities, healthcare disparities, and representation in leadership roles.

Celebrating Excellence

It's truly inspiring to see the rising generation of Black women leaders in America making significant strides across various domains. Activists, educators, entrepreneurs, and politicians are working tirelessly to shape a more equitable and inclusive society. Their collective efforts are paving the way for a brighter future. In grassroots movements, Black women activists are taking the lead in addressing issues such as racial injustice, police brutality, and systemic inequality. They are leveraging their voices and organizing powerful campaigns to raise awareness and mobilize communities. These activists are not only fighting for their own rights but also advocating for all marginalized individuals, promoting intersectionality and inclusivity in their causes.

By providing platforms for dialogue, organizing events, and offering resources, Black female organizations aim to foster a sense of belonging, amplify the voices of Black women, and address the systemic barriers they face. They play a crucial role in highlighting the experiences and contributions of Black women and working toward creating a more equitable society for all.

Black women educators play a crucial role in shaping the minds of future generations. They are committed to providing quality education and ensuring that all students, regardless of their background, have equal opportunities to succeed. By creating inclusive learning environments and incorporating diverse perspectives into the curriculum, these educators are nurturing their students' potential and empowering them to become change agents themselves.

Black women entrepreneurs are breaking barriers and forging innovative paths in business and industry. They are defying stereotypes and creating successful ventures in various sectors, from technology to fashion, and everything in between. Through their leadership, they are not only creating economic opportunities but also serving as role models for aspiring entrepreneurs from underrepresented communities.

In the political landscape, Black women politicians are making waves by advocating for policies that address systemic inequities and uplift marginalized communities. They bring unique perspectives and live experiences to the table, amplifying the voices of those who often go unheard. With their representation, they are challenging the status quo and paving the way for a more inclusive democracy.

Chapter Four

The Power of Black Women in Arts and Culture

4.1 Influential Black Female Artists

In 2015, when American actor Viola Davis became the first Black woman to win an Emmy for outstanding lead actress in a drama series, she gave a powerful speech and said, "The only thing that separates women of color from anyone else is opportunity. You cannot win an Emmy for roles that are simply not there."

What Viola Davis said points to the time in television history when Black characters were few, and sitcoms and shows that included them showed a stereotypical image of Black people. This skewed representation kept Black actors away from displaying their full potential and showing their talent to the world. But her victory proves that through their resilience and hard work, Black women can change the direction of the tide and reach the highest places.

Shortly after making her rousing acceptance speech, Viola Davis gave an interview to a lifestyle magazine and said that at the time of her speech, she was not aware that most people in the audience were able to relate to her speech. And that, at that time, she was not focused on either acceptance or approval—or shame.

In a world where many have endeavored to eradicate racism from society, Viola Davis's Emmy win may not appear significant to you. But the fact that the Emmy Awards were launched in 1949 and that a Black woman could only win the award in 2015, points to racial disparities that Black people face in every field, and yet they remain determined, ever ready to show the world that they are capable of great things.

Viola Davis's victory was remarkable for women of color in general, and the Black community in particular. While she has had her fair share of struggles, she is a shining example of our Celebrating Black Excellence and has impressively carved a place for herself in the Hall of Fame.

In the TV industry, Black characters were nearly non-existent in all-white shows, where rich white families used to have no Black friends or neighbors. The shows that had them would use the characters in insignificant, often demeaning, supporting roles. It has taken years of struggle against oppression for Black women to make a name for themselves and redefine Excellence.

A population that has seen nothing but abject poverty, discrimination, and a complete disregard for their life requires years to come out of the horrors of the past. A generation grew up thinking that they must look a certain way and behave in a certain way to get people to like them. In her book 'Finding Me', Viola Davis shares her struggle with growing up, "po"—a level lower than poor, according to her—and other challenges. She had to face grade-school bullying and had to come back to a home where she had to deal with her alcoholic father.

All these challenges haven't disappeared for most Black communities. Poverty is still rampant, and the system is inherently tilted against them. But the success of Black women, especially those who have passed insurmountable challenges, only shows that anyone can achieve the impossible. It may not be easy, but it is achievable.

Black media personalities have not grown up in isolation. Most of them have had difficult childhoods; they had to search for work at a young age to finance their careers. And yet they have managed to reach where only a few people can reach. They have won the highest awards and created shows that will forever remain in the golden book of American TV.

Inside every young Black woman is Viola Davis, who is determined to change her circumstances and channel her trauma in her work. Inside every young Black woman is Harriet Tubman, who knows that she is not going to make peace with adversity and must stand up to break away from the chains that are holding her back. Inside every young girl is Michelle Obama, who knows that she can make a space for herself in a highly competitive political world and fight for the rights of women and marginalized communities. And inside every young Black woman is Rosa Parks, who is tired of giving in and who wants to be treated with respect and dignity.

Black media personalities and politicians that come on our screens would have remained a distant dream had the heroes of the past not stood up for themselves. History also shows that some struggles start after victories. The end of slavery didn't automatically translate to equal rights and justice. Civil activist, including young college students, had to protest and say loud enough that they wouldn't endure any more humiliation. The road to equality and justice is long and uneven, and it takes lots of guts and courage to keep treading on it—the key is not to back out.

During an era when global leaders actively participated in the slave trade, they could not have fathomed a future where a generation of former slaves would become world leaders. These individuals endured immense suffering, including torture, lack of education, and the denial of basic rights. However, despite these adversities, the Black community emerged from this traumatic history with triumph and remarkable accomplishments.

There is something about the resolve for liberation that makes people passionate and determined. For them, there is no pause—only a goal that they want to achieve. Centuries later, the benefits of the Civil War are still here, allowing people to breathe freely and integrate into public spaces.

4.2 Black Women in Literature and Poetry

A society that embraces fairness and inclusivity can only be created if we amplify the voices and experiences of black women. Representation in leadership positions, decision-making processes, and media platforms is imperative. Implementing policies that address systemic issues such as racial wealth disparities, healthcare inequities, and educational access will be essential in achieving true equality. In the words of Maya Angelou's *Still I Rise:*

Celebrating Excellence

You may shoot me with your words,
You may cut me with your eyes,
You may kill me with your hatefulness,
But still, like air, I'll rise.

The poem is a powerful and inspiring piece that celebrates the strength, resilience, and courage of Black women, and encourages them to stand up and rise above oppression and discrimination.

It is a declaration of the poet's determination to rise above society's hatefulness and discrimination. It is also a call to others to live above the society in which they were brought up. The poem encourages readers to love themselves fully and persevere in the face of every hardship. It is a proclamation of the dignity and resilience of marginalized people in the face of oppression.

It is a beautiful tribute to the human spirit and its ability to overcome adversity. It reminds us that no matter how difficult life may seem, we have the power within us to rise above it all.

The legacy of Black women's struggle persists today, transcending time and uniting generations in the fight against oppression. Their contributions as architects of social change remind us of the ongoing work needed to create a just and inclusive society. By honoring their sacrifices and remaining committed to the principles of past generations, it is important to honor their sacrifices while remaining committed to creating a society that embraces the principles of fairness and inclusivity, we pave the way for a future where equality and justice prevail for all.

*****

And the woman behind the beautiful poem 'Still I Rise' deserves a special mention as well. Maya Angelou played a big role in radicalizing the young generation and teaching them how to embrace their identity and culture. It's common for younger generations to abandon their identity and embrace the dominant culture/identity—that of the ruling elite. But there is something brave about being unapologetically you. And this is what Maya Angelou's poetry espouses.

Maya Angelou had a complicated life where she went through unspeakable tragedies, but her past did not come in her ambition's way. She was always drawn to poetry and would maintain a journal of her writings.

In 1959, Angelou joined the Harlem Writers Guild—a platform that was established to amplify Black voices. She was also a member of the Civil Rights Movement and used her skills to further the cause of the Black community.

In 1969, she published an autobiography that perfectly discussed her early life. Titled 'I Know Why the Caged Bird Sings,' the book connected with many people. The truthful description of what sexual abuse looks like in the book, however, didn't sit well with many schools, which tried to get the book banned. This did not happen. The book became a coping mechanism for most survivors and helped them to address and come out of their trauma. Probably, this relatability helped the book earn 'The National Book Award.'

In 2010, Angelou was also awarded the Presidential Medal of Freedom, the highest civilian award presented in recognition of Angelou's fulfilling career. Her poetry is not only a work of art in English literature, but a portal for all people, especially women who feel alone and in search of an outlet to deal with their past trauma and abuse. Her depiction of what an unequal world looks like is a treasure for those who want to understand structural inequalities and do something about them.

Pause for a moment and go back in time during the slavery period. Now, think about a small girl who is brought to a land miles away from her home. She is now working tirelessly—from the morning to the evening—and has no place to go to share her challenges. Now, if you tell her that years later, Black people will be winning national awards, ruling over the entertainment industry, or stepping inside the White House, will she believe it? Of course not! And it's understandable why your challenges seem too big to handle now. But you have examples of those who come before you and how their circumstances changed. All it takes is one step forward!

For most Black women, Oprah Winfrey, a media personality who successfully ran her talk show for 25 years, is an inspiration. Oprah's candid interviews allowed both her and her interviewees to have meaningful conversations about life, self-help, and other important issues. Her shows were not only a source of entertainment but also a guide for many people looking for answers.

Oprah enjoys a cult-like following, and many people acknowledge the role she has played in helping them turn their lives around. While for some, Oprah can be another TV show host—running a wildly popular program—given the history of Black women, Oprah's accomplishments give courage and hope to young people.

The past is not ideal, and it is filled with abuses that no one would have thought were possible. But it happened. Acknowledging it is one step towards the resolution that this will not happen again.

The retelling of history is not to plant seeds of hatred but to motivate young Black women to think and realize that when those who were subjected to unspeakable horrors can rise above, they can change their circumstances as well. They must firmly believe that the dark night of oppression and inequality will come to an end; the only thing needed is bravery and a promise that no matter what happens, retreat is not an option.

4.3 Celebrating Black Women in Film and Television

Before we go on to explain why we need more Black women in politics, it's crucial to understand how Black women's representation in film and television changes everything. To have a better understanding of this, let's look at the entertainment industry, particularly TV. We chose television because while films and movies are popular entertainment choices, TV is something that is available in every household.

TV is an institution, and what is shown on it matters a lot. For movies, you must make a conscious choice; you must find out which movies are being shown at the cinema, buy tickets, and then watch them. On TV, you may come across a show you otherwise may not have seen while changing channels. On that basis, it does matter what show gets approved for TV and what not. In television, Black people fought hard to make decisions about what image they betrayed of themselves.

Early television was guilty of approving a somewhat limited portrayal of characters who were not white. The depiction of early Black characters had racist undertones, and they were nothing but uninspiring caricatures. This was so because those who were coining such characters had limited views and opinions about the Black community and were not interested in it.

Celebrating Excellence

Then, as time passed, more well-written Black characters appeared on screen. However, this inclusion wasn't enough. Black characters were divided into two categories: too good to be true and violent and irrational. This deprived these characters of the nuances required for fair portrayal.

In the 21st century, this statement seems a little exaggerated. But think about all the old shows that you've watched and name one Black character that existed with white characters but wasn't used as a comic relief or for showing the moral superiority of white people. The most popular sitcom 'FRIENDS' (which still has a global following), doesn't have one Black character in the main group, nor does any of the friends get married to or date a Black character. In one of the last seasons, the main character, Ross, dated a Black professor for a short time.

And so is true for countless other shows. Take the example of 'Frasier' and 'Modern Family'—both shows have won five consecutive Emmy awards—and see for yourself that the two shows don't have one prominent Black character. And they weren't made in the 1960s. These shows are recent, and yet they fail to portray people who are a visible minority in the U.S. And when they (show creators) show these white characters, they indirectly tell you that you have to be exactly like them.

These white characters get to set how one should dress, how family dynamics should be, which sports we should like, and how to celebrate our holidays. But where are the Black people in all of this? Why don't we get to decide what fashion people should follow or what hairstyle should be the next must-have?

Critics say that creative freedom means people cannot be forced into writing characters they don't want to write. But, again, if the industry is filled with people who refuse to give some importance to Black characters, where are all the Black people who want to see their stories on TV supposed to go? Why is it so different to assume that a Black person can be more than a nanny working in an upscale neighborhood or an erratic side character?

And this wasn't happening only in the American entertainment industry? Other countries were also guilty of portraying Black characters that were dishonest and were only added for some comic relief. In Bollywood—India's entertainment industry—the portrayal of most Black characters was quite offensive. But things today have changed quite a lot. For one, creators now think twice before creating a character that could be perceived as offensive by any community. And all of this started happening when people started holding creators accountable for their inherent racism.

The shift in such characters happened in the 1980s, at least in the U.S. We saw 'The Cosby Show' where a Black rich family was shown. This characterization was a thoughtful departure from the predominant portrayal of Black people in mainstream television at the time. However, there were issues that weren't handled in a sensitive manner, and the portrayal (although it holds immense importance even today) had its shortcomings.

We now have a popular television series 'Black-ish'—made almost three decades later—that tries to portray the life of a Black family as truthfully as possible. But one or two shows don't make a difference. The situation is a lot different today, with many creators being truthful about Black characters. Audiences are also getting a look into the many layers of a Black person and their characters are not oscillating between two extremes.

Celebrating Excellence

Diversity is essential in entertainment. There are so many diverse communities in America, and their members deserve to have their stories shown. Through media and storytelling, the Black community was also dehumanized. The laws alone cannot do much with respect to the integration of a community into society. For Ruby Bridges, the law was in her favor, and yet it was a community—a group of privileged white people—who were against her admission to an all-white school. But with television and the arts, people get an opportunity to have a closer look at what it means to be Black in America.

The heartbreaking series 'When They See Us' is a reminder of how dangerous it could be for young Black men whenever a crime is committed in their neighborhood. The fact that five young men, including a minor, were arrested, and kept behind bars for years for a crime they didn't commit speaks volumes of the discrimination that these people faced.

*****

Black women are redefining beauty. For far too long, mainstream media has perpetuated narrow definitions of beauty that exclude Black women. However, Black women have courageously challenged these stereotypes by embracing their natural features and redefining the standards of beauty.

Traditional media was also guilty of showing Black women as voluptuous. Black bodies were often met with lustful gazes to the extent that their bodies became nothing less than sexual treasures. The stereotypical image of Black voluptuous women stems from the slavery period, where they were portrayed as promiscuous while white women were seen as more modest and with sexual purity. This humiliating image of Black women has left deep imprints on our gorgeous Black women who still find it difficult to shake away the generational trauma inflicted by white masters. So, when young Black women saw only white women on screen, they started feeling isolated—as if they weren't capable of being called bold and beautiful.

Thankfully, the dark clouds have now been cleared. We now celebrate luminaries like Lupita Nyong'o and Viola Davis, whose unwavering confidence and grace continue to inspire self-acceptance, self-love, and an appreciation for diversity. You probably think that all these accomplished women may not have had their demons. This isn't the case. Viola Davis has shared, time after time, the struggles she went through and the doubts she had. She also found it difficult to accept the natural beauty of her body.

Understanding the portrayal of Black women on screen is crucial in dispelling any doubts and fostering self-love. Recognizing that you are the protagonist of your own narrative empowers you to share your story, just as everyone else deserves to, and to do so with amplified volume.

In TV, you have people like Ava DuVernay producing and writing 'Queen Sugar' and, of course, one of the most successful TV producers and writers, Shonda Rhimes, and most recently, Quinta Brunson, the creator of Abbott Elementary, the critical acclaim and three Primetime Emmy Award winner.

However, with the various new streaming services and production companies, we are starting to see more Black creatives get deals. And it matters. Take Shonda Rhimes' show 'How to Get Away with Murder.' Viola Davis plays the protagonist. She is a law professor and a fierce one.

Celebrating Excellence

When you see this character on TV, you realize that she's a woman of substance and that she's as realistic as one can be. The character is flawed and yet so powerful. She embraces her negative traits and doesn't shy away from them. This is what was missing from American TV, and Shonda Rhimes ensured that such characters had a visible presence in the media.

Shonda Rhimes also used the show to highlight what it's like to be a Black person in America. She used the protagonist's profession—a lawyer—to explain what it's like for many Black inmates who failed to get empathy from the courts and the jury. There is one remarkable episode in the series where Viola's character represented a Black incarcerated man. To make the jury understand what motivated him to do the crime, she asked all the people present to realize what it meant to remain in solitary confinement amidst absolute silence.

For one whole minute, there is absolute silence to the extent that even audiences may feel a little uneasy. But those 60 seconds were enough to humanize thousands of Black men and women who remain inside jails and receive no sympathy from fellow Americans.

It is one thing to put someone on screen, in front of the camera. It is another thing to let someone—a Black writer/actor like Michaela Coel—have creative control. Something potentially different can happen as Black women are now defining how they are portrayed on the big screen, on television, and in sports. They refuse to be defined by the stereotypes of others. They are also defining how the Black race is seen.

According to the UCLA's 2021 Hollywood Diversity Report, the number of Black characters on TV now matches and, in some cases, exceeds their representation in the general population. However, Black people are still underrepresented among the people shaping the stories, including show creators, directors, and writers. Why is this important? When a Black woman writes a Black woman character—in terms of deciding on her thoughts and her feelings, her personality—you have a true representation of the history of Black women in America. You realize how these women navigated through the past and what their present is like.

It is important for Black women to be more assertive on TV and reclaim the space that is rightly theirs. There have been so many shows and characters that have been nothing less than a stereotypical image of Black people. At a time when there are opportunities to make content that is truthful to the history of Black people, more Black women writers must come forward to tell their stories.

We see American comedian Nicole Byer in 'Nailed It!' where her unapologetically bold commentary is a treat. The brilliant host also uses euphemisms to subtly hint at what Black people used to go through and how they are fighting against oppression. Such women are the stars, and they inspire us to move forward and not let any negative thoughts discourage us from pursuing our dreams.

Also important are many content creators and influencers who have shown the world the potential and power of Black women. From fashion influencers to political commentators, young Black women are showing their potential to the world.

Only Black women's voices can act as a reminder for people about the glorious courage of Black women whose bravery should forever be taught in schools across the world. For so long, Black women have remained hidden from the literature written and the art created to discuss the impacts of slavery on the Black community. While many people have talked about male abolitionists, women's role in the fight against slavery is not mentioned in most places.

Stories told by Black women provide a different worldview, showing the abolitionist and other movements through the lens of Black women. These women have always had great commentary on the politics of the privileged and how people who are concerned about holding their leaders accountable should act. Even on X (formerly Twitter), many Black commentators offer a more nuanced approach toward social and political issues.

Viola Davis has also worked in films that highlight the history of slavery in the U.S. and the treatment Black people went through during the awful period in human history. As audiences learn about the horrors of the past, they learn it straight from people who have gone through abject poverty and know what it feels like to live in an era where leaders turn a blind eye towards you. And as they learn about the resilience shown by Black women and men, they will be reassured that there is light at the end of the tunnel—all people need to do is to fight and try to reach there.

And this is true for all young Black women who are reading this, trying to find some assurances that what they are going through will also end. What the Black community has achieved over the years is incredible, and the determination is apparent in recent fights against inequalities, where they don't mince words when fighting for their rights and raising their voice for oppressed communities and nations across the globe.

All these women mentioned here indirectly encourage you to take full responsibility for your life and live a life that matters; there is nothing greater than fighting for yourself and nothing more respectable than a life of dignity. With that, we move forward to pay tribute to hundreds and thousands of Black women and men who have given a new meaning to the word's perseverance and determination—who have shown the world that living a life that someone else has chosen for you is not the answer and who have shown that rising is always the answer.

We pay tribute to all the women who entered modern politics to ensure that the system doesn't get corrupted again. We also pledge to follow in their footsteps and learn the lessons they taught us years ago. We pay respect to all those who fought against the system, for we know how incredibly courageous it is to swim in waters when the tides are high and against your direction.

And as we do so, we gain the courage to address our battle with the same courage and confidence. The victories of the past didn't occur in a vacuum. They can only be seen as a guiding light for hundreds and thousands of young Black women to motivate them to fight their battles with courage and determination.

Chapter Five

Business and Entrepreneurship

5.1 Black Women Trailblazers in Business

The night of darkness seems long, but the universal law says that at the end of the night, there is a new dawn. And for Black women, this seems to be true. After a long journey of asking for their rights, Black women have finally reached a position where they are now heading big organizations.

For long, Black women remained inside the four walls of their owners' homes. Later, when they got to taste freedom, most of them had to take up low-paying jobs—as caretakers or house helpers. These jobs provided some financial independence to these women, but they were not enough to help them follow their dreams and passions. Now, there has been a visible shift in how Black women choose to lead their lives. For one, they don't have to rely on the crumbs given by others and are now able to strongly assert their demands and work in high positions.

In this new era of inclusivity, where many organizations are vowing to bridge the gender gap, there has been a significant surge in the number of women in the workforce. A 2015 study by First Round Capital concludes, "We know that companies with a female founder perform 63 percent better on average than all-male founding teams." Despite all this, many Black women still face countless barriers when accessing funding.

This is a universal problem; racial and ethnic minorities often face challenges while accessing funding from both private and public organizations. In 2018, U.S. companies raised a total of $130B in Venture Capital funding, (Venture capital (VC) is a form of private equity and a type of financing that investors provide to startup companies and small businesses that are believed to have long-term growth potential. Venture capital generally comes from well-off investors, investment banks, and any other financial institutions), yet only 2.2 percent of that total went toward female-founded companies, and less than 1 percent of the total funding was allocated toward businesses founded by women of color, according to Fearless Fund, which quotes its data from Fortune (2018) and GirlBoss (2019).

Fearless Fund was established to address the gap that exists in venture capital funding for Black women-led businesses and to finally push the needle on the abysmal statistics that drive the current narrative for Black women-led businesses today.

It's important to highlight that recent events have presented new challenges for Black women entrepreneurs. For example, the American Alliance for Equal Rights recently obtained an injunction to temporarily block Fearless Fund, a venture capitalist firm owned by Black women, from awarding its Fearless Strivers Grant exclusively to Black women entrepreneurs. This controversy arises from a dispute over the grant violating equal rights laws, specifically Section 1981 of the U.S. Code, which prohibits racial discrimination in contracting. The case is ongoing, so the outcome and its impact on Black women entrepreneurs remain uncertain.

But despite all of this, many Black women have shown resolve to perform better and single-handedly lead their businesses. From skincare and clothing to NFTs, (NFTs are digital assets that can come in the form of art, music, in-game items, videos, and more. They are bought and sold online.) Black women can now be seen setting up multiple businesses.

For many women, the Covid-19 pandemic provided the nudge they needed to start something of their own. As most companies shut down unexpectedly and the world saw a rise in the cost of living, most Black women put on the entrepreneur hat to make a safe living for themselves.

And when all these women can find a way to set up their businesses and present their startups as profitable in front of dozens of VCs, you can do so. All you need is a strong resolve and will to follow your passion. You may be thinking that it's easy for me to suggest that you can reach your dreams beyond the stars.

It is true that there are many challenges that you may have to go through, but you must understand that you're capable of passing through all those challenges. You have it in you to tell yourself that you will not be demotivated by the challenges that life throws at you, and you have to tell yourself that you'll try harder to become the best version of yourself—to become the person you always dreamt of becoming.

And this is not wishful thinking. You have the power and courage you need to get ahead in life, and you will be successful in achieving your dreams. Telling yourself that you are destined for greater things is the best thing that you can do for yourself.

Black women have gone through years of suppression; they have lived through a period where they were not treated with respect. But they have come so far, and you have to keep the legacy of Black women intact. You are responsible for keeping the names of heroes of the past alive. And you can only do so when you promise yourself that you will exhibit the same courage and passion that those women did.

Your unwavering spirit and resolve are all you need to get ahead in life, and it is that simple. You may have inferred from the examples I shared earlier that most women had that one crucial moment where they decided that they had had enough and that they had to speak up for themselves. You have to channel the energy and courage that those women did and act accordingly.

Once you start walking on the path you laid down for yourself, you'll realize that you have to rise above all self-doubt and criticism—that your dream life and your goals are within your reach.

Even at that moment, you may be thinking that the ship for your better future has sailed. But that's not true. You can change your destiny—whenever you want! You don't have to accept your fate and cry over things that you didn't (or couldn't) have. You must keep reminding yourself that you have to reach your goal—it doesn't matter how long you take, and it doesn't matter what others say. You must spell out what you want and then work toward it.

Celebrating Excellence

Any self-doubts that you may have will hurt only you, no one else. And in this world, you'll find fewer people who'll support you and tell you that you are destined for greater things. Most people will try to discourage you from excelling in your life.

The moment you realize that you're surrounded by people who are pessimists, you should train yourself to recall the heroic efforts of all those Black women who have made a name for themselves in all fields. As soon as you acknowledge the excellence of those women, you'll find the strength within you to achieve your dreams and goals.

5.2 Challenges and Triumphs in Corporate America

So, what does the future hold for Black women? One good thing about the increased representation of Black women is that more people are wary of how certain policies will affect this group. Black women must make these advancements their strength; They must be more vocal about their needs and must highlight how certain policies may be against them.

When people fight for inclusivity, they often tend to be more compromising. At times, getting a seat at the table is all that matters, and even if the position comes with its own baggage, most people consider not making a big deal out of it. But that's not something that young Black women have to carry forward.

In fact, most young people are interested in pointing out the flaws in the system to tell the world that they won't tolerate any discrimination anymore, which is good. It is now up to young Black women to make their voices stronger. The fact that we are living in the digital age where messages can be spread in the shortest time possible, Black women must promise themselves not to tolerate any abuse that is thrown toward them.

It is also vital for Black women to find organizations that are exclusively working to empower Black women. This is important, but such institutions also provide Black women with an opportunity for growth. There's a lot that can be done, and Black women must be more confident about their dreams and passion.

The world is shifting, and young people, especially, are breaking away from the centuries-old biases and negativities. In a world that proudly embraces inclusivity and diversity, Black women must enter all fields and make a name for themselves. The future holds something great for all young women, all you need to do is take that one leap of faith and run toward your goals.

*****

The world is now moving toward artificial intelligence (AI) and machine learning. Whatever skills that you have today may be redundant after a short while. In this fast-paced world, you have to relearn your existing skills and learn new skills. You have to see what's new in the market and how you can benefit from it.

At present, AI is everywhere. From big investors to small consumers, everyone is interested in learning how AI is shaping the world. Countries are holding mega tech conferences to provide companies with a platform to showcase their innovative products. "Tech bros" and "everything tech" are the new buzzwords. Where do Black women see themselves in this era of technological advancements?

Celebrating Excellence

Sadly, the numbers aren't in favor of Black women. The tech industry is generally male-dominated, and women comprise only 26.7 percent of the workforce; Black women make up only 1.7 percent, according to the latest figures available. Those Black women who have entered this field of technological miracles have managed to set up amazing tech startups.

Julia Collins became the first Black woman to successfully combine food and technology. Her startup "Zume Pizza" used robotic technology to make pizzas. The firm was founded in 2015. And although it shut down in 2023, Collins did pave the way for other aspiring women to kickstart their careers in tech.

CEO Jessie Woolley-Wilson of DreamBox Learning is another name that has worked hard to design a math program that helps elementary and middle school students learn math in an engaging manner. It has thousands of math lessons for students.

Then we have Stephanie Lampkin, whose brainchild Blendoor acts as an important tool to combat bias in hiring. Melissa Hanna's Mahmee is another wonderful application that helps new moms obtain prenatal and postpartum care by connecting them to a team of healthcare experts.

So many Black women have been able to set up their startups without any major funding, and while many of them get lucky and manage to run their companies without any financial support, others fail to do so. In that case, it becomes imperative for the government and the relevant authorities to start initiatives that can help Black women claim more space in the tech industry.

5.3 Empowering the Next Generation of Black Women Entrepreneurs

The transformative power of collective action is evident in the work of these Black women leaders. By coming together, they are forming alliances and coalitions that amplify their impact and demand change on a larger scale. This collaboration highlights the importance of intersectionality and the recognition that social justice issues are interconnected. Some of these collaborations will be explained in this chapter.

One inspiring example of the transformative power of collective action by Black women leaders is the formation of the 'Black Women's Leadership Caucus for Racial Justice'. This coalition brought together influential Black women leaders from various sectors such as politics, advocacy, academia, and entertainment. By uniting their voices and resources, they were able to address pressing issues facing Black communities and demand change on a larger scale.

Through their collective action, these leaders amplified their impact by advocating for policies that focused on racial justice, equitable education, criminal justice reform, and economic empowerment. They organized grassroots campaigns, mobilized communities, and utilized their platforms to raise awareness about systemic racism and discrimination.

Their coalition served as a powerful force for change, challenging the status quo and presenting a united front against racial inequities. They engaged with policymakers, corporate leaders, and community organizations to advocate for tangible policy solutions and cultural shifts that would positively impact Black women and their communities.

Celebrating Excellence

Their efforts not only brought about specific policy changes but also inspired a broader movement for social justice. By leveraging their collective power and collaborating with other like-minded groups, they not only amplified their own voices but also created a platform for other marginalized communities to join the fight for equality.

As we look ahead, it is important to continue celebrating and supporting the efforts of the rising generation of Black women leaders. By fostering an inclusive society that values their contributions, we can collectively work towards a future where equity and inclusivity are the norm, rather than the exception.

The Black Women's Leadership Alliance for Economic Empowerment (BWLAEE) is another prominent organization dedicated to advancing the economic status and empowerment of Black women. Founded with the vision of creating a more inclusive and equitable society, the BWLAEE strives to address systemic barriers and promote opportunities for Black women entrepreneurs and professionals.

Through strategic partnerships, advocacy, and targeted initiatives, the alliance aims to improve access to resources, mentorship, and capital for Black women-owned businesses, while also advocating for policy changes that promote economic equality. By fostering networking and collaboration among its members, the BWLAEE empowers Black women to overcome challenges, achieve professional success, and drive positive change in their communities.

This alliance brings together Black women leaders from the business, entrepreneurship, and financial sectors to promote economic empowerment and wealth-building opportunities for

Black women. Through their collective action, they provide mentorship, access to resources, and advocate for equitable economic policies, and aim to close the racial wealth gap and create pathways to success for future generations of Black women.

Chapter Six

Politics and Activism

6.1 Notable Black Women in Politics

States across the U.S. have been dealing with systemic racism, but it is also true that a lot of work has also been done toward racial integration. Remember, we are in a world that has already had its Black first lady. The world has changed quite a lot, and there are so many tools available to dismantle systemic oppression.

Former first lady Michelle Obama's following quote teaches Black women to never abandon their dreams: "Don't ever forget how much power you have."

Every young Black woman carries unbreakable power inside her. You must keep reminding yourself that you're wired to fight against all the tides and all the curveballs that the Universe keeps throwing at you. All you need to do is to have faith in yourself. There's absolutely nothing that you cannot achieve. And this is true for yourself and your family.

The Destiny of Black Women in America

The life and journey of Michelle Obama is inspiring for most women, more so for Black women who see a bit of themselves in her. The former first lady had her set of challenges and disadvantages, and yet she has now become a role model for so many women. She navigated the world stage and handled all sorts of challenges—criticism and whatnot. Her life in politics has motivated many young women to speak up for themselves and not let others' voices drown out their voices.

Young Black women have to trust that there are allies as well. Many accomplished Black women are now focused on helping Black girls and young women find their voice and use their power and potential to turn their dreams into a reality.

The Black Girls Rock platform, for example, was established in 2006 by a former Black model and disc jockey. The movement works to inspire and motivate young Black women who need some inspiration to chase their dreams. From the amazing examples of women of the past to the incredible work done by women today, young Black women can find allies everywhere.

*****

"We did it, Joe." Vice President Kamala Harris' memorable words mark an important turning point in American history. The first female vice president and the first Black person to hold the office, Kamala Harris is a powerful figure in the U.S. today, inspiring hundreds of thousands of people who now believe that they can also enter the American political landscape.

It does take a lot of years for people to change the way the political system is viewed in the U.S. The wave of inclusivity that has now entered the smallest corners of the country will surely lead the superpower to the path of success and progress. Black women have proven over and over that they are a force that can help change the course of history and that they will always be on the frontline of every struggle and movement. And as we celebrate the women of today, we must not forget the political heroes of the past who inspired the heroes of today. Talks about the emancipation of Black women and the civil rights movement are incomplete without the mention of Coretta Scott King. She was a strong voice that highlighted racial issues and economic injustices in the U.S. The widow of Martin Luther King, Coretta was a fierce woman who never minced her words when she called out those responsible for the economic suppression of the Black community.

She was committed to the cause of economic justice. Her unnerving commitment could be gauged from her participation in a labor strike that was held days after the funeral of her husband, who was assassinated in Tennessee in 1968. She openly registered her protest against the Vietnam War. Her open criticism also put her under FBI surveillance for several years. Throughout her life, Coretta spoke about racism in the U.S. In 1969, she had the honor of being the first non-Italian to receive the Universal Love Award. She documented her life in the memoir 'My Life with Martin Luther King Jr.'

Women like Coretta held on to the foundations of the Civil Rights Movement. They also paved the way for future generations who saw themselves struggling to claim the rights that were trampled on by different governments. The dawn of an equal life in the U.S. has not been completed. Black women routinely face discrimination and must work extra hard to get their voices heard.

Pioneer politicians like Shirley Chisholm began her professional career as a teacher. She served as director of the Hamilton-Madison Child Care Center until the late 1950s, then as an educational consultant for New York City's Bureau of Child Welfare. In 1968, Chisholm became the first African American to earn election to Congress, where she worked on the Education and Labor Committee and helped form the Black Caucus.

In 1972, she made history again by becoming the first Black woman of a major party to run for a presidential nomination. After serving seven terms in the House, Chisholm retired from political office.

Condoleezza Rice is another fierce Black woman whose work as a politician has allowed several young Black women to enter the world of politics. She served as national security adviser from 2001 to 2005 and secretary of state from 2005 to 2009. Condoleezza Rice created history in 2004 when she became the first Black Secretary of State.

*****

Even in the present day, it remains a challenging task for women to openly express their frustration and declare that they've reached their breaking point. It demands considerable courage for women of color to firmly stand on the side of history and refuse to echo the narrative propagated by media moguls and business tycoons, which often works against minority communities.

To date, Black women face forced expulsions and other discrimination at work if they dare to speak for the growing injustices. But these women, like the brave women before them, keep standing tall, unfettered by what others throw at them.

The persistence of racist undertones in the world is evident through the case of Meghan Markle, a renowned American actor who married into the Royal Family of the UK. Her revealing interview with Oprah Winfrey sheds light on the deep-rooted racism within the UK's political structure. The taunts she endured and the biased treatment she received from the British media highlight the fact that people still tend to judge individuals based on the color of their skin.

However, what is phenomenal is to see how Meghan Markle stood up for herself and refused to tolerate bad behavior. She made history by walking away from a life of royalty and chose to live away from the spotlight that was constantly against her. She decided to live her life on her terms, and she has shown the world that you have a choice to put your self-respect over everything else and keep your head high.

*****

The impressive journey of Black women points to the fact that sometimes, all it takes is one moment of courage. We all are familiar with the remarkable American activist Rosa Park from Alabama. Now, let's imagine a different scenario. Let's go back in time and imagine a bus where the seats reserved for the whites were full; a white man boarded the bus and found no place to sit. The bus driver asked the Black people to give up their seats, and all of them agreed without any protest. What could have happened then? Nothing.

Things would have remained unchanged, and we don't know how long it would have taken for the Black community to protest against racial segregation. It might have taken more time to put an end to racism. This is how fear affects your plans. That feeling of fear pushes you away from your dreams for months or years. Sometimes, all you need is to get up and say no to the injustices you face or to get up and do something for yourself.

One decision by Rosa Parks created history. It was that one moment that changed people's behavior, and it was that one moment that made those who were in charge of the country's governance pay attention to such an important issue.

Rosa Parks' refusal to get up—a seemingly casual decision—helped the Black community across America. She was arrested for this decision because, at that time, it was rare for a Black person to not do as told. But Rosa Parks remained firm.

According to her, "People always say that I didn't give up my seat because I was tired, but that isn't true. I was not tired physically, or no more tired than I usually was at the end of a working day. No, the only tired I was, was tired of giving in."

And this is the power of not giving up—of not giving in. Opportunities will come your way when you make a firm decision that you are not going to back down. It is quite common to see people losing the spirit to move forward—the situation, the tests, and the difficulties become too much to handle. In that time, it is understandable that you get demotivated, but you have to keep reminding yourself that better days will come. It may not happen instantly, but your efforts will lead you to your desired results.

Celebrating Excellence

Rosa Parks' refusal to say no to the bus driver didn't instantly convert into a win. She was arrested for not giving up her seat. But she refused to be treated like an inferior, and her fight finally allowed lawyers to challenge the disrespectful racial segregation rules in the state. And this fight inspired other Black students to demand fair treatment.

In 1960, Black college students took center stage when they refused to leave the lunch counter without being served their meals. This happened in Greensboro, North Carolina, and led to the Greensboro sit-ins. Protesters were met with aggression, and some were arrested.

But this didn't stop people from standing up for what was right. They announced a boycott of all segregated lunch counters, and eventually, the owners had to give in. The four students who started the protest and held their ground were finally served at the same counter where the entire episode had started.

Around four years later, the country saw the passing of the Civil Rights Act of 1964, which was a revolutionary legislation aimed at tackling inequality. The law provided equal employment to all, ordered authorities to ensure the integration of public facilities, and added limits to the literacy tests required for voting.

Now, let's take a moment to understand the gravity of the situation. We have come so far from the period of slavery, where Black women and men were treated as sub-humans. In the 1800s, people who were born into poverty wouldn't have thought that years later, they would be fighting for their rights and winning it.

All that was needed then was determination and an unshakeable will. Our history is packed to the brim with stories of resilient and courageous women and men who took full responsibility for their lives and fought for them. And that is what one needs to excel—be it a curveball thrown at you or any other limitations, when there's a will, there's always a way!

And it should be a reminder that these victories were not free of the blood and sweat of Black women's rights activists. It is easy to read about them now, but given the political environment of the 1950s and the 1960s, it was indeed hard for all Civil rights activists to demand their rights courageously. It was the time when Black women had to walk on eggshells, and still, when it came to fighting for themselves, they didn't think twice.

Success knocks on the door of those who are not afraid of trying. If you know you are capable of doing something, but you are not doing it out of fear of the unknown, you are not only hurting yourself, but possibly generations to come. Things that happened in the past or things that still affect you cannot dominate you forever. Of course, there will be barriers throughout your life, but you can wire your brain to find a way out of them.

The human spirit is unbreakable, and the inherent nature of humans is to keep trying. Everyone feels good and motivated when they get to have a smooth ride, but it takes courage to act when things are stacked against you. The reason why the names of the women of the past have remained alive is because they did the unthinkable—they didn't let their circumstances define them.

And while all members of the Black community joined the fight for their rights and freedom, Black women had to go through unimaginable levels of pain. A Black activist whose struggle can never be forgotten is Fannie Lou Hamer, who became a household name with her struggle for equal economic opportunities for people from her community.

The turning point in her life came in 1961 when a white doctor performed a hysterectomy on her without her consent. In those days, this was normal. Called "Mississippi appendectomy," this forced sterilization was a way to reduce the Black population—a way to ensure that they remained in the minority. But this dark night had to meet its end. Fannie Lou Hamer didn't accept her fate but gathered the courage to bring the much-needed change. While she couldn't go back in time to ensure that her body wasn't violated, she vowed to protect the rights of the Black community so that such incidents wouldn't happen again.

In a democracy, it is important to have leaders that understand your problems and issues. In those times, the U.S. Congress didn't have many Black representatives. Fannie Lou Hamer decided to do something about it. And her political struggles deserve mentioning to understand how certain struggles are continuous. One must be mindful of how the system is not beneficial for them so that they can do something about it.

For example, Fannie Lou Hamer was deeply angered when Black people were denied their right to vote based on the literacy tests. She decided to do something about it. Her political activities gained momentum, and in 1963, she and other activists were arrested as they were found guilty of sitting inside a "white-only" bus station restaurant. Hamer and her fellow women activists were taken to a jail in Winona, where they were subjected to brutal torture. The beatings that Hamer endured gave her lifelong injuries—leg and kidney damage and a clot in her eye.

The Destiny of Black Women in America

But this incident was also pivotal in increasing Hamer's public image, allowing her to co-launch the Mississippi Freedom Democratic Party (MFDP), which played a revolutionary role in countering the mainstream parties' efforts to block Black participation in the electoral process. Hamer's political journey was strewn with blockades and other deterrents. In 1965, she became one of the first Black women to stand in the U.S. Congress protested the Mississippi House Election of 1964, for which she had applied for candidacy but was barred from the ballot.

Now, fast forward to 2008. In August 2008, Michelle Obama delivered a speech at the Democratic Convention saying, "When my husband, Barrack Obama, embarked on this incredible journey to the White House, we knew that change was possible. We believed in the power of unity and the strength that lies within each one of us. And today, as I stand here, I can see that the change we longed for is no longer just a dream, but a reality within our grasp."

The dream that matured in 2008 took years to become a reality. For a population that had gone through oppression and injustice, the ascent of a Black man to the highest power corridors was nothing less than a surprise, where they took a long moment to finally accept that someone who looked like them could be the head of the state, could make decisions for his people, and could turn the country into an inclusive place.

The dream that matured in 2008 would have remained a distant reality had civil rights activists not taken to the streets in the 1950s and the 1960s. It could become a reality only when Rosa Parks refused to stand up or when Fannie Lou Hamer decided to fix the loopholes in America's political system.

*****

Celebrating Excellence

Not only are Black women destined for the greater good, but Black girls are also showcasing their skills at all possible levels, establishing their names as high-accomplished people. Take the example of 14-year-old Anala Beevers, one of the three Black geniuses in the world. The young girl was only 10 months old, she could identify every letter of the alphabet, a feat that left many astounded. Shortly after her remarkable alphabet feat, Anala's intelligence continued to impress.

By the time she was five years old, Anala could recite the names of all North American states and their capitals from memory. This mind-boggling accomplishment showcased her extraordinary memory recall and understanding of complex geographical concepts at an age when most children are still learning basic reading and writing skills.

Anala's incredible intelligence is not just limited to her impressive memorization skills. Testing revealed that she possessed an IQ of over 145, firmly placing her in the highly gifted range. Her high IQ score suggests advanced problem-solving abilities, exceptional critical thinking skills, and a remarkable capacity for learning and assimilating knowledge beyond her years.

Anala Beevers' story serves as an inspiration to both parents and educators, emphasizing the importance of recognizing and nurturing children's unique abilities and talents from an early age. Her parents played a crucial role in recognizing and supporting her exceptional aptitude, providing her with the resources, encouragement, and educational opportunities necessary to thrive academically.

The story of Anala Beevers also highlights the significance of early stimulation and engagement in a child's intellectual development.

It underscores the importance of providing a rich learning environment that encourages curiosity, exploration, and cognitive growth.

As Anala Beevers continues her remarkable journey, it will be fascinating to see how her exceptional abilities shape her future. With her extraordinary intelligence and thirst for knowledge, she is poised to make a significant impact in various fields as she grows older.

Anala Beevers' incredible intellectual abilities have captured the attention of the world since she was just a baby. Her early accomplishments, such as alphabet recognition at 10 months and memorizing all the North American states and capitals by the age of five, showcase her exceptional cognitive aptitude.

Anala's story is a testament to the potential of young minds and the importance of nurturing and fostering their unique talents. As she continues to mature, she serves as an inspiration to all, reminding us of the remarkable possibilities that lie in our future and the future of Black women.

6.2 Black Women's Impact in Grassroots Movements

Black women's struggle has not been without significant challenges and adversity. Despite facing intersecting forms of discrimination based on race and gender, they have exhibited remarkable resilience. From enduring the horrors of slavery to battling systemic racism and sexism, Black women have persevered against overwhelming odds.

Celebrating Excellence

Their resilience is evident in their unwavering commitment to community building and grassroots activism. Through organizing, mentorship, and support networks, Black women have nurtured spaces for empowerment and uplifting others. By fostering social cohesion and advocating for change at both the individual and systemic levels, they have played a pivotal role in dismantling oppressive structures.

And this brings us back to where we started. Black women in politics. Like TV, politics is also guilty of excluding Black women. For so long, Black women relied on the kindness of leaders who never walked a day in their shoes. While the political system is the same throughout the world, minorities struggled to get some space in the power corridors of the country, and the situation for Black women used to be worse.

The situation, however, did a favorable turn, and many Black women realized the importance of becoming part of the system so that they could talk about the issues they faced in a more effective manner. The 2020 election, in that regard, marked a major milestone in Black women's political leadership. Kamala Harris became the first woman and the first Black person to become the country's vice president.

When people of color find themselves in important positions, minorities can expect that their problems will be discussed with more compassion. And in the 2020 elections, besides the ascent of Kamala Harris, other Black women also found success across other levels of office, in addition to playing pivotal roles in voter mobilization and voter turnout.

Glynda Carr of Forbes Women notes that these findings reflect trends that are slowly but powerfully transforming the political landscape: "In 2020, we saw another year of historic developments, coming after a record number of Black women running for office in 2018. We already knew that Black women would power the road to the White House and the road to 2020, but this data shows that Black women candidates are stepping off the sidelines as viable candidates with voters' support. Black women are converting electoral power into political power."

Her statement further goes: "Black women are a powerful force in the American political system, and their political power at the polls and on the ballot continues to grow and is increasingly recognized as the force it is. When Black women run for office, they not only challenge biased views of who can or should lead but also disrupt perceptions of electability."

Twenty-four Black women currently serve in Congress, all serving in the U.S. House. In addition, two Black women serve as non-voting delegates. All Black congresswomen are Democrats. For a brief period at the start of the 117th Congress, Black women hit a new record for congressional representation; between January 3, 2021—when new members were sworn in– and January 18, 2021—when Kamala Harris resigned her U.S. Senate seat—a record 26 Black women served in Congress.

When Representative Marcia Fudge (D-OH) left office in March 2021 to become secretary of Housing and Urban Development, the number of Black women in Congress dropped to 24, which is still one more Black woman than served in Congress at the end of 2020.

Black women are 4.5 percent of all members of Congress, 9 percent of all Democrats in Congress, 16.8 percent of all women in Congress, and 39.3 percent of Black members of Congress. They are 5.5 percent of all members of the House, 20.2 percent of all women in the House, 41.4 percent of Black members of the House, and 10.9 percent of Democrats in the House. No Black women currently serve in the U.S. Senate.

"Black women's underrepresentation is due in part to the fact that they face additional hurdles, including disparities in financial resources and outdated biases about what leaders look like in this country. "Black women continue to have to push through and jump over institutional obstacles and manufactured barriers. And that includes raising money and raising money early," adds Carr.

She further explains, "This makes it even more important to step up and support these candidates with our time, money, and votes. As report author Kelly Dittmar, Associate Professor of Political Science at Rutgers University–Camden and Director of Research at CAWP, told me, "Once we have defined Black women's underrepresentation as a problem, it's up to all of us to try to solve it. That means supporting Black women at all stages of the campaign process, from candidate recruitment and emergence to the ballot box on Election Day. Citizens can support Black women on the campaign trail with their time and their money, and they can support Black women at the ballot box with their vote. And due to biases—often among long-time party influencers—about Black women's electability, that support needs to come early and often to debunk myths of un-electability. Especially for those who spent much of the past 18 months on social media or elsewhere calling on others to 'listen to Black women' or 'support Black women,' it's time to translate those hashtags into action that can actually enhance the support infrastructure for Black women to run and win elective office."

These Black women, alongside many others, left an indelible impact on the struggles for freedom, equality, and civil rights. Their bravery, resilience, and determination continue to inspire generations today.

*****

Black women throughout history have played a crucial role in shaping the fight against oppression and injustice. From the time of the Civil War to the Civil Rights Movement and beyond, their contributions and resilience have left an indelible mark on society. In this summary, we will explore the enduring legacy of black women's struggle, recognizing their sacrifices and emphasizing the ongoing importance of creating a fair and inclusive society.

Black women have been the architects of social change, leading the charge against deeply rooted systems of oppression. Their fight for equality has encompassed various aspects of society, including racial justice, gender equality, and socioeconomic empowerment. From abolitionists like Sojourner Truth and Harriet Tubman to civil rights activists such as Rosa Parks and Fannie Lou Hamer, Black women have consistently challenged the status quo.

Their immense contributions extend beyond the realms of activism and include the arts, literature, and academia. Figures like Maya Angelou, Audre Lorde, and Toni Morrison used their platforms to highlight the experiences and struggles of Black women, bringing their stories to the forefront of societal consciousness. By amplifying their voices, Black women have paved the way for future generations to continue the fight for equality and justice.

To better understand why this representation matters, try to give the answer to the following questions: Is it possible for us to use a term to define years of abuse and humiliation Black women faced when America was engulfed in the flames of slavery?

Is it possible for us to explain, as realistically as possible, what these women felt when they were subjected to hatred and blatant discrimination? Living during times when your existence itself was seen as nothing less than a crime, is it possible to understand what it was like to break the shackles of oppression and carve a destiny of your own?

Can we imagine a world where people—living and breathing people were not seen as people with aspirations, dreams, and lives? The world has seen an era where traders would discuss the sale of humans, not the newest products. It seems tragic and nearly nauseating to acknowledge that the world and its leaders had the capability at some point to treat people as subhumans, to divide people based on their race and the color of their skin. That the wave of industrialization was so high and dense that it dwarfed all the concerns for human rights and humanity in general.

And since we don't have definite answers to these questions, it becomes abundantly clear why Black women's voices matter. They matter because only they have the agency to talk about the power imbalance. It doesn't mean that other communities may not have gone through gender-based violence, but for a community that has closely witnessed oppression, it's important for its women to have a powerful voice, instead of relying on others to speak up for them.

6.3 Advocacy for Social Justice and Policy Change

Black women and girls are disproportionately affected by socioeconomic issues that diminish their quality of life and have a devastating effect on the well-being of Black families and communities. The Congressional Caucus on Black Women and Girls gives black women a voice in making crucial decisions on the policies that impact them while also providing a framework for creating opportunities and eliminating barriers to success for black women. The caucus was inspired by Ifeoma Ike, the co-founder of Black and Brown People Vote, and a collective of six other women involved in the #SheWoke committee which is comprised of leading black women activists who consistently advocate for their rights, including Ike, Nakisha M. Lewis, Tiffany D. Hightower, Shambulia Gadsden Sams, Sharisse Stancil-Ashford, Dr. Avis Jones-DeWeever and Sharon Cooper.

Collectively, these women, along with members of Congress, helped to launch a caucus that will aim to address issues important among black women, like economic equity, education, wellness, and safety, among others.

The caucus aims to achieve success by creating public policy that eliminates significant barriers and disparities experienced by black women.

The formation of the caucus marks a hugely significant moment for minority communities as it is the first of 430 registered congressional caucuses and member organizations that are specifically designed to make black women and girls a priority.

Equally important is to have a look at the judicial system and equal justice under the law. Three Black women — two prosecutors and a judge — are in unenviable positions to lead former president Donald Trump and this nation in lessons on democracy, accountability, and the rule of law.

Celebrating Excellence

New York Attorney General Letitia James, Atlanta-based District Attorney Fani Willis, and U.S. District Judge Tanya Chutkan have been bombarded with threats, often racial or sexualized. A Texas woman has been arrested for a death threat against Chutkan; an Alabama man has been charged with targeting Willis.

It is concerning that their gender and race would be used as an excuse to ignore wrongdoing and Trump's authoritarian plans for a second presidency. He insinuates that the prosecutions are part of a vast conspiracy to replace white people.

In 2022, there were only 33 Black women — less than 2 percent — among the nation's 2,100 elected chief prosecutors, according to the Reflective Democracy Campaign. And even with President Joe Biden's successful push to get more women of color into judgeships, there are 59 Black women — 4 percent — among the 1,409 sitting federal judges.

That these three Black women involved in such high-profile cases underscores this nation's progress. And it instills hope that it will live up to the promise: "No one is above the law." And reiterate the Destiny of Black Women in America

The history of Black women from slavery, the Civil War, and the Civil Rights movement is a complex and multifaceted journey marked by resilience, resistance, and the pursuit of freedom and equality.

During the era of slavery, Black women endured unimaginable hardships, including physical and sexual abuse, separation from their families, and forced labor. Despite these immense challenges, many Black women found ways to assert their agency and resist oppression, often through acts of defiance, storytelling, and nurturing supportive communities.

The Civil War, fought from 1861 to 1865, brought significant changes to the lives of Black women. With the Union victory and the abolition of slavery, Black women experienced newfound freedom, although the challenges of racism and discrimination persisted. Many Black women seized opportunities to establish their own businesses, educate themselves and their children, and actively participate in social and political movements advocating for civil rights.

The Civil Rights Movement of the mid-20th century further propelled the fight for equality. Black women played integral roles in the movement, serving as leaders, organizers, and strategists. Figures such as Rosa Parks, Fannie Lou Hamer, and Ella Baker made significant contributions to the fight against segregation, voter suppression, and other forms of systemic racism. Their activism and resilience paved the way for important legislative victories, such as the Civil Rights Act of 1964 and the Voting Rights Act of 1965, which aimed to dismantle racial discrimination.

Throughout history, Black women have triumphed over adversity, leveraging their strength, intelligence, and determination to challenge systemic injustices. Their contributions to society, both in the face of adversity and in the pursuit of justice, have been crucial in shaping the progress towards equality and civil rights for all.

The success of Black women has greatly contributed to the progress and empowerment of the Black race over the years. Black women have made significant strides in various fields, including politics, academia, business, arts, and entertainment. Their achievements have served as powerful examples and sources of inspiration for others within their communities.

Black women's accomplishments have challenged stereotypes and shattered barriers, demonstrating that talent, intelligence, and leadership are not limited by race or gender. By breaking through these barriers, they have paved the way for future generations, providing representation and opportunities for other Black individuals to thrive and succeed.

Furthermore, Black women have been at the forefront of social justice movements, advocating for equality, civil rights, and racial justice. Their involvement and leadership have played a pivotal role in shaping these movements, raising awareness about systemic issues, and demanding change.

The success of Black women has also sparked important conversations about intersectionality, recognizing that race and gender intersect to create unique challenges and experiences. By addressing these intersections, Black women have contributed to a more comprehensive understanding of social issues and fostered a more inclusive approach to activism and policymaking.

Overall, the achievements of Black women have been instrumental in advancing the Black race. They have inspired and empowered their communities, challenged societal norms, and laid the foundation for a more equitable future.

We, as Black males -- sons, husbands, and friends -- deeply appreciate the unwavering support of our black females and recognize the indispensable role they have played in shaping our nation. Their resilience, fortitude, and unwavering spirit have been instrumental in overcoming numerous obstacles.

It is crucial to acknowledge that celebrating the achievements of Black women does not diminish or undermine the struggles and accomplishments of Black American males in American society; there have been many. Instead, it is important to emphasize the significance of recognizing and honoring our mothers, sisters, and all women for their remarkable successes.

By appreciating the unbreakable bond between Black women and men, and through our collective support and collaboration, we can truly understand and value the united front that has propelled both genders towards greater heights of achievement and equality.

Chapter Seven
Health and Wellness

7.1 Black Women and Healthcare Disparities

Education has always been a cornerstone in breaking barriers, and black women have played a pivotal role in championing knowledge and empowering future generations. Dr. Mamie Phipps Clark was a pathbreaking psychologist whose research helped desegregate schools in the U.S. Over a three-decade career, Dr. Clark researched child development and racial prejudice in ways that not only benefited generations of children but changed the field of psychology.

In 1934, Clark graduated high school and received multiple scholarship offers from Historically Black Colleges and Universities (HBCUs). Despite the expense of sending a child to college, a burden made worse by the Great Depression, and the limited college options for African Americans, Clark's parents were determined she would get a degree. Clark went to Howard University in Washington, D.C., on a merit scholarship. She knew she wanted to help children.

After graduation, Clark was unable to find an academic job despite her accomplishments. Clark first took a job as an analyst at the American Public Health Association and then as a research psychologist at the U.S. Armed Forces Institute. In both jobs, she felt she was in a "holding pattern." She then became the testing psychologist at the Riverdale Home for Children, a refuge for homeless girls. That work made her realize there was a lack of services for African American children in Harlem.

She advocated for more services and resources but was met with silence from the city government and others. Taking matters into her own hands, the Clarks started the Northside Center for Child Development in 1946; it was the first and only organization in the city that provided mental health services to African American children. Northside offered psychological testing, psychiatric services, social services, and academic services and became a center of activism and advocacy for Harlem and its residents. Clark ran Northside until her retirement in 1979; the center continues today.

Based on her graduate research, Clark conceived of and implemented "The Doll Test" in the 1940s. In it, the Clarks looked at 253 African American children aged three to seven: 134 attended segregated nursery schools in Arkansas, and 119 attended integrated schools in Massachusetts. Shown four dolls (two with white skin and blonde hair, two with brown skin and black hair), the children were asked to identify the race of the doll and which they wanted to play with.

Overwhelmingly, the children wanted to play with the white doll and assigned it positive traits. The Clarks concluded that African American children formed a racial identity by age three and attached negative traits to their own identity, which were then perpetuated by segregation and prejudice. It was a pathbreaking study.

Due to this work, Clark served as an expert witness, testifying in many school desegregation cases. In one, she testified against her Ph.D. advisor, Henry Garrett, who argued in favor of segregation. In the landmark case Brown v. Board of Education (1954), which ended school segregation in the United States, NAACP lawyers used Clark's research and expert testimony in their successful arguments. While history books credit Kenneth with "The Doll Test," he even said, "the record should show [it] was Mamie's primary project that I crashed. I piggybacked on it."

Clark's study is a testament to the racial inequality children face at educational institutions. And the U.S. of today is not completely free from all these obstacles. What has changed, however, is the country's will to keep changing and embracing inclusivity. Young Black women have a lot of avenues to explore, and they should not let society hold them back.

It's true that life doesn't always work out in our favor, but many people have indeed learned the art of resilience and getting back up after being knocked down. It's particularly powerful when one believes that behind every principle lies a promise. This belief can be especially empowering for Black women pursuing their dreams. The heroes of the past didn't necessarily follow a unique formula; instead, they often adhered to principles and ultimately found their well-deserved rewards. It's a reminder that sticking to one's principles and persevering can lead to success.

Hard work does pay off, and it does make a difference. It is true that there will be people with privileges. But their privilege can take them to a certain point, and how well they perform depends on how they make use of their talents and power.

The reason why the period of slavery continues to be remembered in the 21st century is not merely to recollect the atrocities a specific group endured. Rather, it is because the stories of remarkable Black women who faced numerous obstacles and lacked many opportunities persist today. The concept of Black Excellence serves as a powerful motivator and should be continually shared to inspire individuals, emphasizing that they too, can pursue their dreams and attain them through the unifying force of unity.

*****

Trauma is a dangerous thing, and like a parasite, it keeps clinging to the body of its host. It doesn't matter how much a person tries to break free from the horrors of the past, trauma has a way to come back, like a stray that doesn't leave your place if you feed it once.

Most Black women have had to deal with certain traumas throughout their lives, the effects of which are still visible. Researchers, over the years, have found that those women who had early exposure to Jim Crow laws (which legalized racial discrimination in southern U.S. states until the mid-1960s) can develop certain health complications. And the effects of this trauma can be deadly. For example, research by Nancy Krieger, professor of social epidemiology, highlights that "among U.S. women currently diagnosed with breast cancer, being born in a Jim Crow state heightened black women's risk of being diagnosed with estrogen-receptor negative breast tumors, which are more aggressive and less responsive to traditional chemotherapy."

Celebrating Excellence

And that's not all! Many Black women also face discrimination by health professionals. Most women have complained that health practitioners often dismiss their complaints and ask them to trust what they're doing or "let the medication work." And as the concerns of these women are dismissed, they suffer from avoidable health complications.

A majority of Black women are entrapped in the shackles of economic deprivation, which makes it even more difficult for them to access quality healthcare. Black women are also more prone to suffer from diseases like hypertension, cardiovascular diseases, and certain types of cancer. They're also twice more likely than white women to develop diabetes over the age of 55 or have uncontrolled blood pressure.

All these diseases are a direct result of the environmental factors that most Black women are exposed to. Imagine this: for a Black woman who is hardly getting by, arranging funds for childcare services becomes extremely difficult. They are then forced to admit their children to childcare centers that are not high in the ranking. Families that live paycheck-to-paycheck have additional stressors to deal with. And when these women reach the age when their kids are grown up and financially independent, their bodies refuse to be on their side. The years of trauma and stress make the body frail and vulnerable to most diseases.

And for some Black women, the date with trauma happens at a very young age. Most young girls face sexual abuse at a very young age—the abuser is often a close family member, stepfather/uncle/father/grandfather). Girls as young as 13 years old often get pregnant after rape. While there are institutions like Planned Parenthood that help these girls to abort unwanted pregnancies. But the procedure did take a toll on them.

And this mental toll is not limited to the trauma they go through. Most girls tolerate the abuse and taunts of their mothers, who blame them for the horrible things they endured. It takes years for these girls to shake off the burden of the trauma and ensure that the memories of what happened in the past don't come in the way of their success and a chance at a healthy life. Naturally, all of this is not easy. And in the process of collecting and fixing their broken pieces, most women miss out on a lot due to past abuse.

7.2 Promoting Health and Wellness in Black Communities

Black communities have several disadvantages. Their economic deprivation and the fact that they have the system against them often create health challenges for them. But things are changing, and most people are now realizing that it's essential to help marginalized communities deal with their problems in a healthy manner. There are certain methods that can be used to help Black women tackle their health issues easily and with care.

In today's world, the most important tool is technology. Several health apps can be used to connect Black women in need with a top-rated healthcare professional. Apps that track a patient's vitals, like blood pressure, can help doctors adjust the dosage accordingly. Access to real-time data means that doctors can make decisions quickly, ensuring that a patient always has access to top-notch care.

Health practitioners should also be trained in a way to reduce the bias they hold. It is important for doctors to listen to patients' complaints, regardless of how general they sound. In fact, healthcare professionals should be trained to identify social conditions that may have led to a Black woman's health issue. Once doctors have a better understanding of the triggers that affect a woman's health, they are in a better position to advise their patients on how they can tackle such triggers.

Black women's health is an important factor that mustn't be ignored. It is unfair to thousands of women that they must deal with avoidable health problems just because they happen to be born at a time when people in power were against them. It is also quite unfair to realize that most women become victims of those men whose extremist tendencies are triggered by the environment they were exposed to and the challenges they had to endure.

Taking women's health in a light manner is extremely dangerous, and it is on every one of us to play our part in ensuring that Black women have access to the best healthcare. In that regard, training people from the same community can also work perfectly. Why is that so? People who are familiar with the challenges that Black women go through on a daily basis can better assist them in case of emergencies. For medical professionals to have some perspective of the challenges that women go through is a plus point. Training Black medical professionals so that they can give back to their community can be a great first step in ensuring that Black women have equal access to healthcare.

On a larger scale, it is essential to work collectively to address health inequity. Black women don't have to rely on self-medication or treatments done by non-professionals just because they don't have the financial means to access healthcare. There should be more funds at the government level to help these women gain access to healthcare in a respectable manner.

*****

There are certain coalitions that were set up to address the health challenges that most Black women face. The Black Women's Health Imperative Coalition is one of them. This coalition focuses on addressing the health disparities experienced by Black women. By combining the expertise of healthcare professionals, community organizers, and activists, they advocate for better access to quality healthcare, reproductive justice, mental health support, and research funding.

Their collective action has led to increased awareness about the unique health challenges faced by Black women and the need for targeted interventions. The 'Black Women's Health Imperative Coalition' is a collective effort dedicated to addressing the health disparities that Black women face.

This coalition brings together professionals in healthcare, community organizers, and activists who collaborate to advocate for improved access to quality healthcare, reproductive justice, mental health support, and research funding. By leveraging the collective expertise and influence of its members, the coalition works towards raising awareness about the unique health challenges that Black women encounter. They aim to highlight the need for targeted interventions to improve overall health outcomes within this population.

Through their advocacy efforts, the Black Women's Health Imperative Coalition seeks to empower Black women and ensure that their healthcare needs are prioritized and addressed. They work towards creating a more equitable and just healthcare system that considers the specific concerns and experiences of Black women.

Another important organization is the Black Mothers Matter Alliance (BMM), which is a powerful movement and organization that emerged in response to the ongoing struggles faced by Black mothers in various communities. Founded in 2015, the BMM aims to elevate the voices and experiences of Black mothers, spotlighting the unique challenges they face within a society plagued by systemic racism and social injustice. This alliance strives to address issues such as maternal mortality rates, healthcare disparities, and unequal access to resources.

This coalition works towards improving maternal health outcomes and experiences for Black women. By amplifying the voices and experiences of Black mothers, they advocate for policies that address racial disparities in maternal healthcare, support culturally competent care, and promote maternal well-being. Their collective action has resulted in increased awareness of the unique challenges faced by Black mothers and a platform for systemic change.

By advocating for policy changes and promoting awareness, the BMM works tirelessly to ensure that Black mothers and their children receive the support, protection, and opportunities they deserve. Through their collective efforts, the Black Mothers Matter Alliance plays a crucial role in amplifying the voices of Black mothers and fighting for a more equitable and just future for all.

7.3 Addressing Mental Health in Black Women

Do you ever feel that some weight is placed on your head or on your chest? So many people wonder what it feels like when you cross a storm. How does it feel when you finally defeat your demons? The answer is that the day after is not that rosy.

The heart and mind of a broken woman is a mystery. The fights that women face and the barriers that they break take a toll on them. As a result, when they're finally done fighting their battles, they feel an indescribable feeling of something missing. The toll that the fight takes on a woman's mental health is dangerous, and yet many Black women are expected to behave as if nothing happens—as if the battles they won or silently fought were personal affairs and they should not let themselves get sunk into the memories of the past.

Many accomplished Black women have shared that the trauma of the past often doesn't go away and keeps returning at odd hours, forcing the person to look at the scars of the past.

Now imagine what could be the state of mind of a person who has yet to fight their battles—someone who hasn't had the opportunity of understanding what their triggers are or why they react in a certain way.

Mental health is a complex issue, and it must be handled properly. Women who have unresolved mental health issues often face critical problems when they set out to discover their path to success. They struggle academically and at the workplaces. And even though more people are now mindful of other people's mental health and education institutes and workplaces are making conscious efforts to ensure that people who are dealing with any mental health issues have access to care and help if they need it, the situation still needs years to improve.

There are many employers that still carry some bias and prefer not to work with people who disclose their mental health issues. For most Black women—given the expensive price tag that mental health care carries—going to therapy is not an option.

It becomes important for community leaders to have affordable therapy options for Black women so that they can have access to a trained professional who can empathetically listen to their troubles and suggest a solution. Women should also be encouraged to seek therapy whenever they feel that the weight of their traumas or stressors is making it difficult for them to live their lives in peace.

Black women have come a long way, but they still have certain battles to fight. In that fight, what most people can do is make it easy for these women to get the care they need. It is not easy, but at least the first step must be taken so that these women can also enjoy the beauty of life in its true sense.

Chapter Eight
Role Models and Inspirational Figures

8.1 Icons and Trailblazers

Black women's incredible journey is not limited to education, politics, and entertainment, but these incredible women have managed to enter all fields—and have made a good name for themselves. Black women in sports continue to enthrall the world with their impeccable skills.

Historically, Black women in sports faced double discrimination due to their gender and race. Many Black American female athletes have emerged as trailblazers in their sports over the years, from track and field and tennis to figure skating and basketball.

The struggles and hard-won glory for pioneers such as Alice Coachman, who made history at the 1948 Olympics in London in the high jump competition when she leaped to a record-breaking height of five feet, six and 1/8 inches to become the first Black woman to win an Olympic gold medal.

Celebrating Excellence

Althea Gibson, between 1956 and 1958, became the first Black player to win the French Open, Wimbledon, and the U.S. Nationals.

Wilma Rudolph was an American sprinter who overcame childhood polio and went on to become a world-record-holding Olympic champion and international sports icon in track and field following her successes in the 1956 and 1960 Olympic Games.

Lynette Woodard made history by becoming the first female member of the Harlem Globetrotters and, at age 38, began playing as one of the oldest members in the newly formed American women's professional basketball league, the WNBA.

And who can miss Serena Williams? One of the greatest tennis players of all time, with 23 Grand Slam singles titles, Serena is the GOAT (Greatest of All Time). And while she is a beast in the field, she has had her fair share of discrimination. Her outburst during the U.S. Open final in 2018 exposed her to racist comments. But Serena held her head high and did not let any negative commentary affect her.

Other exceptional Black athletes are Simone Biles—a dominant gymnast who has won numerous medals, including multiple Olympic golds. Naomi Osaka—a professional tennis player and Grand Slam champion known for her activism. Allyson Felix—a track and field sprinter, one of the most decorated athletes in U.S. history. Cori Dionne "Coco" Gauff—an American professional tennis player. She has won six WTA Tour singles titles, including a major at the 2023 U.S. Open, and eight doubles titles.

Have you ever found yourself standing in front of a mirror without a mock trophy in your hand and giving an acceptance speech to an imaginary audience? Do the stories of these incredible women tell you that you can achieve your dream? All these women are just like you—whatever you are feeling or whatever you are going through, they have had to face that. These women have made their name in a society that was not as inclusive as others.

It took years for someone like Viola Davis to become a top actor of all time. It took Oprah Winfrey years of hard work to reach the top place. But they did work toward their dream every day. Regardless of the circumstances and regardless of the systemic oppression, every day, they woke up and worked toward a better life, toward their dream.

*****

The young girl that you see in the mirror, holding a mock trophy, is the image of the future who will have the opportunity to share her story with the entire world. Black women have come out to talk about their life struggles, how poverty and other systemic inequalities have clipped their wings, and how they will continue to fight for what's theirs. It takes unparalleled levels of perseverance and grit to stand up after falling over and over. It takes patience and nerves of steel to push back the trauma of the past and be determined to prove to the world that they can do wonders.

We have seen the courage in the #MeTooMovement, founded by Tarana Burke, a global social movement that aims to end sexual violence and empower survivors. Burke, an American activist and business executive, who coined the phrase "me too" in 2006, was a Black woman who documented the abuse that many women went through at workplaces, public places, and homes. The movement allowed politicians to finally talk about the gender inequalities that Black women go through. Because of the work of the earlier heroes, Black women have found a voice to document their grief and find a way for the correction of past mistakes.

For Black women, the writings of Angelou and the legacy of Tubman serve as a powerful testament to the undeniable truth that resilience and bravery can indeed pave the way to positive outcomes. Their stories resoundingly proclaim that simply waiting for oppressors to have a change of heart while remaining idle is not an option. Instead, they implore Black women to rise up and be the catalysts for change, disrupting the oppressive status quo and demanding the attention and respect they deserve.

The U.S. of today is vastly different from the U.S. of the 18th and 19th centuries, but the U.S. of today is also harrowingly similar to the norms that were acceptable then.

The fight to reverse voting rights in the Supreme Court is another ongoing issue that has implications for democracy and civil rights. The Voting Rights Act of 1965 was passed to protect Blacks from discrimination in voting by enforcing federal oversight of state election laws. However, in 2013, the Supreme Court struck down Section 4 of the Voting Rights Act as unconstitutional, which required certain states and jurisdictions with a history of voting discrimination to get approval from federal authorities before changing their voting laws.

Since then, several states have enacted laws that critics say are designed to suppress or disenfranchise voters of color or other marginalized groups. For example, Texas has passed a law that bans mail-in voting and limits early voting hours[8], which could make it harder for people of color to cast their ballots during the pandemic. Other states have also passed laws that restrict voter registration access or purge voter rolls based on inaccurate data.

In response to these challenges, civil rights advocates have called for Congress to pass legislation to restore and strengthen Section 4 of the Voting Rights Act or create new provisions to protect voting rights at the federal level.

The death of George Floyd is a reminder that supremacists can be anywhere, and that there are some people who have no respect for human life. In that case, all people have is their ideology and a will to fight for their rights.

The "We Can't Breathe" movement is another striking reminder that Black people's unity and collective action is essential to fight against the status quo. and while many Black people have made it to important positions, the fight will stay the same. Because the fight now is not against any one community, but against a particular mindset that supports the annihilation of Black women and men; the fight is against the impunity people enjoy when they commit crimes against people of color, and the fight will carry on until all such ideologues are not broken.

The success of the movement also shows that things are moving and that winds of change are covering the country. Good things happen only when people show a commitment to change and resolve to not let their fears destroy their will to do better and say no to injustices. There are so many Black women around us who are fighting their battles silently so that others don't have to face any discrimination. All these women are our heroes, and all these women make this world a better place.

*****

Bravery and courage are destined for good fortunes. The victories of these women have paved the way for countless other women to face their circumstances with smiles on their faces. There is no place in the world where people can have it all without any struggle—both inner and external. And the barriers that you routinely face in your journey towards your goal are there to make your personality even stronger.

Celebrating Excellence is a great way of understanding that you are capable of achieving great things, regardless of your circumstances. There are so many Black women throughout history who did the unthinkable and proved to the world that they could change the course of their fate. Their selfless work and sacrifices have made it possible for you and others to get up and fight for themselves.

And this "Excellence" of resistance that Black women showed is not limited to a particular event or against a particular system. Resilience is an important trait that all humans have; it's their way of saying that they won't accept any injustices and inequalities. You can apply these values in your life as well.

It is also possible for you to read about the lives of remarkable women of the past and think that the issues that you're facing today are inconsequential. But that's not the point of sharing these stories. The lesson that we need to learn from their story is that only you are responsible for changing your circumstances.

And while it is important (and essential) to have a strong support system, you have to be ready to fight your battles all by yourself. The heroes of the past did not wait for anyone to fix the issues that were pushing them back, farther away from their dreams.

One interesting trait of humans is that they want to see the good in people; they have the urge to be met with kindness and love. But the world is not designed that way. And this is not only about how people are divided by race, gender, or ethnicity. But within the same communities, you may have to deal with jealousy, envy, and other bad things you want to stay away from. But what does that represent?

It is rather simple: the world is not a bed of roses, and your journey is supposed to be full of challenges. There is a saying that a diamond gains its shine from the pressure it goes through. Every bad thing that happens to you may have a lesson for you.

In life, there are several instances where we think that our life doesn't have any purpose anymore. Imagine this: you are a high school student and have everything planned. You know which course to take and which jobs to apply for after your four-year degree. But as you start your academic journey, you realize that things are not going according to plan. Such are things that can set you back; you lose the will to move ahead and want to stay in bed all day long.

This is understandable. When it seems that things are not going as planned, you lose all hope, and the will to try. But the past has so many examples for you to realize that giving up is not an option. You cannot let one bad thing dictate the course of your life, no! Everybody has their own challenges and tests. No one has it all, but what matters is how you're going to deal with the roadblocks laid out in your way. And the manner in which you tackle your problems makes all the difference.

When we're young, we have an insane amount of optimism and a strong belief that things will rarely be any different than our plan.

Celebrating Excellence

But life is more than that. And a part of chasing our dreams means to fight against all odds firmly and strongly. The reason why these incredible women are role models for so many people is that they hold their heads up high in the face of adversity.

Reaching your milestone when everything is in your favor is super easy. Real growth happens when you're knocked down and are forced to get up on your own. The resilience of women of the past shows that determination and an unshakeable spirit can help people get whatever they want. And you have to channel the same energy when you're met with any challenge. You have to tell yourself that you can do it—that you can face the hard times and come out victorious.

There are so many examples that show how far Black women have come, but one incredible example is that of Claudine Gay, the first Black woman to become president of Harvard University.

Yes, this is a moment of pride for so many young Black women and girls who try to search for their role models in top positions. That a Black woman became president of an Ivy League university is bigger than anything else. Now compare this with the time when Black women had no access to education or the time when half of America came out to protest the admission of a Black girl in an all-white elementary school. Resilience does pay off!

Claudine Gay's promotion as president may not have been possible had Black women and girls of the past not fought for their rights. When we hit rock bottom, when everything seems almost impossible to achieve, depression creeps in. And in that moment, we let pessimism get the better of us. But by doing so, we're only hurting ourselves.

The Destiny of Black Women in America

If we keep telling our brain that we're destined to settle for less, the brain will not create any urge inside us to do better. But this must stop. Claudine Gay's example is the best to explain how your hard work can lead you to places that were supposed to be out of your reach. Who would have thought that a Black woman would become president of America's most prestigious university?

But do you think this could have been possible had Ruby Bridges not shown courage and perseverance? She was met with criticism and hate at a young age, and she might have thought about not pursuing her education. She might have thought that there was nothing that could change how society saw her. But she didn't let the hard time push her away from claiming what was hers.

She did not waiver; she didn't get the admission forcefully. She was given an opportunity to prove that she was capable enough of studying at a better educational institution, and she made the most of it.

In order to truly navigate through challenging situations, one must possess an unwavering resolve. While it may not always be possible to change the circumstances or people surrounding you, you can stand firm in your decisions. It is crucial for young women to recognize the importance of this concept as it reflects the remarkable progress America has made in respecting and upholding diversity. This progress acknowledges that education is a fundamental right, granting individuals the autonomy to pursue knowledge and skills in a manner that aligns with their personal beliefs, values, and learning styles. However, it is vital to acknowledge that racism and discrimination still exist in the country. Nevertheless, just as bridges are constructed over mountains and streams, it is essential to build your own path and overcome these challenges. Many strong Black women have

Celebrating Excellence

cleared the way for you, serving as a testament to the resilience and determination necessary to succeed.

While it is true that instances of discrimination against Black people still persist, what truly matters is the extent to which the country takes action against such injustices. Fortunately, we have witnessed in the past that both the government and the public are committed to holding those accountable who engage in discrimination based on color and gender. It is important to acknowledge that these remarks are not meant to belittle the challenges and hardships you may have experienced or are currently facing. However, it is essential to draw strength from past stories and channel your courage towards moving forward. Remember, things do improve over time. And there is a principle that should guide you in this process.

At the end of your hard work and dedication is a promise—a reward that you'll get whatever you're looking for. Victory is supposed to be yours; all you need is to tell yourself that you will go all out to claim what's yours, without getting intimidated by the challenges that your journey comes with. And when you start telling yourself that you won't take no for an answer and that you will decide your fate by yourself, you'll see that everything has started falling back into place.

The high tides of pessimism can demotivate even the most optimistic ones. But you have a responsibility towards yourself, and that is not to get affected by the difficulties that come your way. When women of the past can take the responsibility of claiming what was theirs, you can do so. There are so many battles that have been fought by those who came before you. All you need to do is to take their legacy forward and promise yourself not to let the bad times destroy you or your potential. Celebrating Excellence is yours to claim.

In fact, quite recently, in July 2022, a controversy sparked on social media where a mom accused the characters at Sesame Place, a popular theme park located in Langhorne, Pennsylvania, for ignoring her two daughters (who were Black) and shaking hands with a white child standing next to them. This incident, understandably, attracted the ire of a number of people who were appalled at the insensitivity shown by the characters at the park. The incident also led to a formal statement and a lawsuit against the park.

As Rosa Parks said: "I was a person with dignity and self-respect, and I should not set my sights lower than anybody else just because I was Black." And when we learn about incidents like the 2022 one, it gets even clearer that standing up for yourself and our race only leads to people and institutions correcting their mistakes.

8.2 Unsung Heroes and Local Legends

Apart from Harriet Tubman, there were other fierce women who were at the forefront of a harsh war against the oppressor—powerful oppressors who had created a world order that favored them over others. Given the structural injustices that people were exposed to, the victory was phenomenal and rightly deserves a place in the golden book of history.

Mary Prince was another fierce anti-slavery activist who used her pen to document the abuse the enslaved population went through for years. What happened inside the closed door of palatial mansions remained trapped inside the walls of larger-than-life architecture, but Mary Prince provided a window inside the lives of enslaved Black women.

Mary Prince also opened her eyes to an unfortunate and unequal world where she was sold to slave owners along with her mother. At an age when she should have been receiving gifts and other souvenirs, she was "gifted" to the daughter of her slave owner.

Over the years, she was sold to different people. Not only was she supposed to do physically tiring work, but she was also subjected to sexual abuse by her owner. The years of neglect and abuse had no end in sight—at least for some time.

While the efforts to get her unconditional freedom remained underway, Mary started documenting the tragedies, difficulties, abuse, and trauma she endured throughout her life. Mary's autobiography 'The History of Mary Prince' worked as a voice of the voiceless. In her famous quote, she strongly objected to the notion that slavery was beneficial for some. She said, "I have been a slave myself — I know what slaves feel — I can tell by myself what other slaves feel, and by what they have told me. The man that says slaves be quite happy in slavery — that they don't want to be free — that man is either ignorant or a lying person. I never heard a slave say so."

Mary's documentation of her life also acts as a reminder for people in today's world, who are forever reminded of the terrors that people in power can unleash against the economically weak. The stories of these women are important because they show the power of the human spirit. It doesn't matter what happened yesterday—and it doesn't matter what happened years ago—the important point is to do something about it. Mary Prince was a child when she was sold to a slave owner and brought miles away from her home. And yet, she had the unquenchable thirst to break the chains of slavery and fight for herself.

There are times when you must be the first one—the first in the family to pursue your dream career, the first one to buy the house, the first one to say no to any injustice, and the first one to break the cycle of trauma and violence. Throughout history, Black women have shown that they are not less than anyone; they have used their potential for themselves and their community.

Maria W Stewart is a well-known name today -- the first Black woman to become a political writer. She gave speeches to loud audiences at a time when no woman (Black or white) would address large gatherings. Her words explain her bravery: "Shall I, for fear of the feeble man who shall die, hold my peace? Shall I, for fear of scoffing and frowns, refrain my tongue? Ah, no!"

Maria had a fire in her, a passionate desire for liberation that made her do the unthinkable and prevented her from getting trapped in the established norms of society. Maria was not born into slavery, but when she lost both her parents at the tender age of five, she had to work as a domestic servant.

Maria knew her public speeches were against the established norms of society. She had famously said, "The frowns of the world shall never discourage me," indirectly telling people that they should not let the voice of others' opinions drown their inner voice. She was aware that Black people held immense talent. She argued that "give the man of color an equal opportunity with the white, from the cradle to manhood, and from manhood to the grave, and you would discover the dignified statesman, the man of science, and the philosopher."

Celebrating Excellence

The brilliance of these women suggests that sometimes all it takes is to speak up—at the right time. That one moment where you get up and say, "I am going to do something about this," leads you to the path to progress and achievement. Had Harriet Tubman not decided to escape from the house of her slave owner, hundreds of slaves would not have been free. Years of abuse and violence can come to an end if people show courage.

8.3 Inspiring Stories of Resilience and Achievement

Why does education hold importance for Black women? It is not only about one community; education is important for anyone who wants to move ahead. But for Black women, it holds a lot of importance mostly because their degrees are sometimes their only window to a world full of opportunities. At present, Black women are among the most educated groups in America.

And this is not a small achievement. The fact that so many Black women acknowledge the importance of education goes to show that it is something that young Black women and girls should see as their superpower—something that will help them fight the injustices of society.

This should also act as a great motivator for all those young women who find themselves confused about which way to choose. In this highly competitive world where systems are designed in a way that several communities will forever remain at the receiving end of injustice and discrimination, it's essential to navigate your path wisely.

Hard times are an integral part of our lives. This is true not only for those living in America but also for those in the rest of the world.

If you look at the situation outside of the U.S., you'll find that there are countless people who have some struggles to deal with, and they do so patiently and with determination.

Bad times are not here to stay for long, and if you give in, you'll hurt only yourself. We often ask for a guiding light, someone who can hold our hands and show us the right path. And as we grow up, we realize that the hand that is supposed to lead us to success is ours. You may not realize it now, but you do have a lot of potential to fight against bad circumstances and build a successful path for yourself.

When we read the stories of the women of the past who fought heroically, we learn the lessons of patience and perseverance. We may not have to deal with the circumstances they went through (and thankfully, the situation is quite better than what happened in the past), but we have to build the skills needed to weather all the storms that come our way.

In this world, emotional intelligence is significant. It is essential for everyone to work on themselves to become more mature and learn the ability to filter out all the negativity and toxicity they face and remain focused on their goals.

Toni Morrison—the first Black woman to win the Nobel in literature—had an important thing to say to all those who encountered (or still encounter) racism in their life. She said: "The function, the very serious function of racism is a distraction. It keeps you from doing your work. It keeps you explaining, over and over again, your reason for being. Somebody says you have no language, and you spend twenty years proving that you do. Somebody says your head isn't shaped properly, so you have scientists working on the fact that it is. Somebody says you have no art, so you dredge that up. Somebody says you have no kingdoms, so you dredge that up. None of this is necessary. There will always be one more thing."

Toni Morrison also took the responsibility of telling the stories of Black women on her own. She didn't ask for any help or rely on other writers to acknowledge the pain that Black women went through. Gradually, her prose provided a window to the outside world to understand the complexities of the life of a minority, especially women of color.

She was also quite honest about her writings and why she chose to write about the Black community. In one of her famous quotes, she says: "I never asked Tolstoy to write for me, a little colored girl in Lorain, Ohio. I never asked [James] Joyce not to mention Catholicism or the world of Dublin. Never. And I don't know why I should be asked to explain your life to you. We have splendid writers to do that, but I am not one of them. It is that business of being universal, a word hopelessly stripped of meaning for me. Faulkner wrote what I suppose could be called regional literature and had it published all over the world. That's what I wish to do. If I tried to write a universal novel, it would be water. Behind this question is the suggestion that to write for black people is somehow to diminish the writing. From my perspective, there are only black people. When I say 'people', that's what I mean."

Toni Morrison's successful life shows that Black women can achieve whatever they set their minds on; they don't have to settle for less or compromise on their dreams. The confidence that she showed in not only her writing but also her interviews should be a lesson for all young women who cower in the face of unjustified criticism and try to sugarcoat their opinions. Accomplished Black women have shown—time after time—that you don't have to be sorry for being yourself.

*****

All young Black women are full of potential, and they have to believe in themselves and promise themselves that they will not let the negativity destroy them. If you ever find yourself unsure about where life will take you, you have to tell yourself over and over that you'll be the one who will decide which place is worth settling in. When you look at yourself, you have to search for the Toni Morrison inside you, the Shonda Rhimes inside you, and all the brave and courageous Black women who have shown the world that they are worthy and that they can move the mountains if they have to.

There's another quote by Toni Morrison that will elaborate on the power of taking things into your hands. She says: "If there's a book that you want to read, but it hasn't been written yet, then you must write it."

What does that mean? It means that you have to start thinking about yourself and decide how you want your life to be. So, suppose if you don't know any Black woman who is great at sports, you can become one. If senior Black girls at your school have not participated in competitions like dancing or singing and you know that Black girls are capable of becoming the best dancers or singers, you can be that star.

Just because someone hasn't tried something different or new doesn't mean that you shouldn't give yourself a try. How many times have you pushed back your dreams because of what society has defined for Black girls and women? How many times have you decided not to make one channel on YouTube or any other video-sharing platform because you're not sure if anyone will be interested in listening to what you have to offer?

Do you know what the consequences of not doing anything are? You get pushed back so many months and years! That one moment when you decide not to act on your gut feeling, you lose days and months—all this time that may have been spent on focusing on your skills and polishing them.

Validation from the outside (the environment in which you function) is good and heartwarming, but you have to stop relying on what others say and focus on yourself. You have to be true to yourself. And, yes, everybody loves living a stress-free and carefree life; everyone wants to not deal with a fractured system, but you can either run from it or learn from all those hardships and become a well-rounded person.

You read about all these women, and what's the first thing that comes to your mind? Do you think that all these women had some special powers that helped them turn the direction of the tides? They were women driven by goals, determination, and conviction. Their secret power was their desire for freedom and equality.

They were ordinary women with some extraordinary ideas. Abolitionists who were on the frontline of the freedom movement had one idea: that they would be free. And they worked toward it, without thinking about the problems that they would have to deal with. They listened to their hearts and set out on a journey that wasn't easy.

The Destiny of Black Women in America

The thing about past events is that they are told in a way that we (even if we make a conscious attempt at not doing so) fail to understand the gravity of the situation. For example, today, when we talk about slavery, a lot of people might see it from the lens of today. It is hard to fully understand what the circumstances were.

And this is not something wrong. Now that the world is more civilized, the horrors of the past seem unbelievable. But you have to really go back in time and think of a situation where you had no phones or no other means of communication. And yet, a Harriet Tubman emerged and used the underground tunnels to transport many Black slaves to their final destination—to freedom. You know you read these stories today, and you see so many people paying tribute to the heroes of the past; you see people around saying loudly and proudly that had they been there, they would have helped Tubman and women like her who walked on the path to freedom.

But things were not rosy for women who decided to carve a path to freedom. You see, there were both men and women who were against the very idea of the freedom of the Black community. So many people were out to get them, arrest them, and punish them for their courage. And yet these women did what they did.

And you'll be rather glad to know that you have a Harriet Tubman inside you as well, who can fight against the bad times and emerge victorious. All you need to do is believe in yourself and understand that you can be a champion as well!

You see, there was a time not too long ago when Black women were not allowed to go to all-white schools or have their opinion. And today, we are living in a world where opinions of Black women

Celebrating Excellence

celebrities matter, where so many politicians want Black women to be on their side—that's the power of being true to yourself.

We have seen how the Black women of today don't fear what the world will say about them. Take the example of Meghan Markle, who got married to Prince Harry in 2018 and became part of the Royal Family. Sections of the English press treated her badly and ran malicious stories, but she stood her ground. She faced all the criticism, lies, and bad press with a smile on her face and took a stand for herself and her children.

What she did was something extraordinary. She decided to move away from the Royal Family, said goodbye to a life of luxury and royalty, and chose a life away from the bad press. And even before that, she had successfully made a name for herself in the entertainment industry. She was one of the few Black women who effortlessly carried the success of a television show (in her case, Suits) on her shoulders. And her story is full of challenges. Standing up to a press that was critical of her wasn't easy. She received criticism from people who used to be on her side. But she didn't let any of that deter her.

She once said: "Make a choice: continue living your life feeling muddled in this abyss of self-misunderstanding, or you find your identity independent of it. You push for color-blind casting; you draw your own box. You introduce yourself as who you are, not what color your parents happen to be."

You know all these women have walked so that you can run! They have made it easier for you to navigate your surroundings and confidently give answers to people who have doubts about your ability. You don't have to let other people push you back.

And do you know what happens when you let negative thoughts get the better of you? You stop doing what you're meant to do. You start doubting your abilities, and that's when things start going downhill. You think—wrongly—that whatever achievements you had were by accident, by chance. This is where you must be mindful of all the criticism. It is good to listen to constructive feedback and bring the change necessary, but it's extremely dangerous to let other people's opinions drown out your voice, your passion, and your will to move ahead.

And any talks about celebrating Black women's excellence are incomplete if we fail to mention bell hooks—a remarkable feminist writer—who, through her impeccable poetry and prose, made a strong point against discrimination. Throughout her life, she had been a strong proponent of advocating that people should not judge others based on their race or gender. She also fought fiercely against the discrimination that many Black people faced in the workforce, where they were appointed to low positions deliberately.

For you to succeed in life, you have to be confident! You have to tell yourself that you have whatever it takes to get ahead in life. And you can now be sure that you're not alone—that you have the success and wisdom of hundreds of Black women who came before you and fought a majority of battles for you.

Chapter Nine

Future Prospects and Challenges

9.1 Building on Successes and Momentum

Most educationists in the past had already understood the importance of motivating Black women to get an education. In 1881, two educationists, Sophia B Packard and Harriet E Giles, set up a college for Black women, which is now called "Spelman College."

The primary goal of the education institution was to bring social change through empowering young Black women. The college, located in Atlanta, Georgia, became the most sought-after place where many Black women got a chance to acquire the skills they needed to excel in life. When the school was first established, it had a class strength of 11 students and was then named the Atlanta Baptist Female Seminary.

Three years after its inception, in 1884, John D. Rockefeller had a chance to visit the school. He was thoroughly moved by the vision of the school's leaders and was impressed by the institution's commitment to women's education. He was so moved by the initiative that he decided to donate a generous amount to the institution.

This money helped the management to expand its business. The institute was renamed "Spelman Seminary", a name given to honor the wife of John D. Rockefeller, Laura Spelman Rockefeller. The generous amount from Rockefeller went a long way to help the institute expand its horizon.

The college continued providing high-quality education to Black women and instilling in them the skills needed to get ahead. In 1924, it transformed into a four-year college. Lucy Hale Tapley helped the college gain its accreditation, and it was finally named "Spelman College." This remarkable shift became a turning point for the college, which started providing more academic opportunities to students while simultaneously maintaining its strong commitment to community engagement and social justice.

This college turned out to be a lifeline for Black women who found a safe space to hone their skills. Spelman College was blessed in the sense that it had the best leaders who worked tirelessly to expand the institute and keep offering quality education to Black women and empowering them to become the next big leaders.

In 1987, the college had its first Black woman as president. Dr. Johnetta Betsch Cole headed the college with utmost dedication and left behind an unforgettable legacy. Under her tenure, the college had impressive community outreach programs. The college also had a significant and visible increase in faculty recruitment and campus development.

Celebrating Excellence

Spelman College has consistently ranked among the top liberal arts colleges in the nation, known for its strong foundation in the humanities and sciences. The institution's commitment to academic excellence is complemented by a deep dedication to service and social justice, producing graduates who are prepared to make a difference in their communities. Spelman's alumni have gone on to excel in various fields, including business, academia, the arts, and public service.

As we approach the 150th anniversary of Spelman College in 2031, the institution continues to expand its legacy. The curriculum offers diverse academic programs targeted at producing leaders who are equipped to address the complex challenges of the modern world.

Spelman maintains a steadfast commitment to empowering Black women and fostering a supportive community. The college actively promotes inclusivity and equity on campus, cultivating an environment where students can confidently pursue their dreams.

Spelman College has a long and storied history that continues to shape the lives of Black women. From its humble beginnings to its status as a leading liberal arts college today, Spelman exemplifies the power of education and the transformative effect it can have on individuals and society. As we celebrate the achievements and contributions of Spelman College, we recognize the enduring impact it has had and will continue to have on generations of women seeking education, empowerment, and equality.

The college's remarkable legacy goes to show the impact of education on people's lives. Any steps made in the education system should well be regarded as small seeds planted in the garden of growth and excellence. The care shown today will reap benefits for years to come. For Black women, institutes like Spelman

College are nothing less than a blessing, as this education center strives hard toward bringing social change by empowering Black women.

*****

Over the years, Black women have also realized that a career in education plays a vital role in acquiring a higher education. This is so because they believe that a teacher or an administrator who has an understanding of how racism and discrimination affect students' academic lives is well suited to lead a generation of students who have to deal with several roadblocks in their academic journey.

This doesn't imply that only people of color can teach students from the Black community, but this merely reiterates the notion that the absence of Black voices in the management or administrative departments at schools and colleges carries the risk of ignoring the plight of students. It is quite common to see that most policymakers at education institutions are divorced from the lived experiences of many Black students and fail to understand how certain decisions can affect them or push them away from their academic goals/targets.

In that sense, it becomes extremely important for people from within the community to work at high posts and be a strong voice in the policymaking process to ensure that final decisions and rules are not inherently against marginalized communities.

Even though things are getting better in America and more leaders are paying attention to the principles of inclusivity, divides within the system are still there and will continue to take a unified effort to completely go away. False accusations against Black people are still common. When the high positions are devoid of any representation by the people of color, the accused gets deprived of any chance to prove their innocence. We saw in the Emmett Till case where one unverified accusation led to the horrible lynching of a boy. Would things have been any different had we had an officer who understood the nuances of such accusations? These are questions that will remain a mystery for a long time.

But it is heartening that more leaders are now advocating the inclusion of Black women in positions of authority. They can help handle tense circumstances in a better manner. All in all, it's extremely important for young Black women and girls to pay attention to education and use their degrees as a stepping stone toward a life of success. The world is full of examples of high-achieving Black women who have shown the world their potential.

You can also reach your goals if you start education as a powerful tool that can help you follow your dreams and passion. And as you look around you, you'll see that there are many educationists who are working towards empowering Black women. Spelman College became a guiding light for Black women who set out to search for academic opportunities. Spelman College, like many others, is waiting for young Black women who are passionate and want to get ahead in life. Don't let the invisible chains of society's regressive thoughts stand in your way of progressing toward a rewarding future.

9.2 Continuing to Address Intersectionality

It wasn't easy—the fight to get their presence noticed, the fight to claim what was theirs, and the fight to become a respectable member of society. In today's world, the way Black women have asserted themselves in all fields of life is impressive and doesn't

The Destiny of Black Women in America

give a hint of what might have happened years ago. But behind the happy faces of accomplished Black women lies a story—a tale of blood and tears, dejection, and heartbreaks.

Over decades, Black women have been able to carve a society where they are seen for what they are—where their talents are respected and where young Black girls can see themselves in movies and TV shows as the lead characters, doing everything fiercely. But this utopian environment was not always the fate of Black women who had to pass insurmountable obstacles to ensure a kinder society for their future generations.

It is easy to look at and applaud the successful Black women of today. It is easy to say that while the past was tragic, it is important to move on. But by not acknowledging the adversity Black women faced at the hands of slave owners, society becomes guilty of dismissing the struggles of a people who, for most parts of their lives, received nothing but abuse and neglect.

After the abolition of slavery, Black women had to start a civil rights movement (again, decades later) to say a loud no to racial segregation and assert their presence—to demand respect (something which should have been given to them without them asking for it). For years, Black women remained deprived of opportunities that may have given them a lucrative future. This treatment was partly because most people assume them to be eligible for only subordinate roles.

Years of oppression are not washed away soon, and most people who had had the history of owning slaves and making them work all their lives for nothing found it difficult to shake off their prejudices and extend the respect Black women deserved.

Celebrating Excellence

As someone who was in an endless cycle of poverty and lack of opportunities, many Black women had to take up low-paying jobs to survive and ensure that there was food on the table for their children. But this, again, was not a pleasure cruise. The jobs that they were hired for had their set of challenges.

These barriers were visible, and most women were aware of them. Luckily, the strong and fierce women of those times were ready to struggle for the betterment of their future generation. There are countless examples of Black women who navigate through the obstacles-laden education system to provide quality education to fellow Black women.

And who would've guessed that the person who worked tirelessly for the education of Black women would be someone who was born into slavery? Mary Jane McLeod Bethune was a remarkable woman whose name will forever stay in the Book of Gold and who will be remembered as a guide to humanity.

Mary Jane McLeod Bethune's reason for setting up an educational institution had its roots in a personal tragedy. After her marriage ended, she found herself responsible for the upbringing of her only child. Determined to give her son a good future, she set up a school which eventually—based on her tireless efforts—became a college. Throughout her life, she worked tirelessly for racial integration at educational institutions and ensured that all children had equal opportunities for education, regardless of their race.

Although the period of slavery is laced with atrocities, one silver lining of it was an important realization. Black women realized that if they wanted to go ahead in life, they had to attain quality education and be prepared for what life has to offer. This realization

The Destiny of Black Women in America

led to other discoveries—how the U.S. education system is designed to favor rich and wealthy white students.

Education is the key to a better future, and it is remarkable how many Black women tried to set the stage for their future generations. Although a lot has changed over the last few decades, education for Black children is still a tricky subject. A student's chance of going to a good school depends on the zip code of the area they're living in.

Zip codes determine schools within a district. Not all public schools impart the same level of education. In fact, schools that are in neighborhoods that are densely populated by Black families often have early-career teachers. Such schools also have low resources, and Black children are deprived of the vital skills required to get ahead in their lives.

It would be dishonest to say that things have been perfect for the Black community or that they can now reach their goals easily. But what should not be lost amid all this is the fact that many Black women—and men—attained an education at a time when the system had countless roadblocks. The circumstances were against them, but they didn't let their situation determine their fate. They took the responsibility for determining which way their lives would go, and they were quite successful at it.

Today, Black women who second guess themselves should think about all the heroes of the past, who made the most of whatever little they had to have a future better than the circumstances they were born into.

Celebrating Excellence

Struggles of the Black community anywhere in the world deserve accolades, but in the United States of America, the term Celebrating Excellence has a distinct meaning. Here, Celebrating Excellence signifies the strength and resilience of Black women and men who defied (and continue to defy) all odds stacked against them to reach their goals. And this is because for close to a century, Black people lived as slaves across the U.S.

In modern discourse, the Civil Rights Movement of the 1960s is considered a turning point for the Black community. But the struggle of Black people started years before that. The U.S.—the land of opportunities—was once a prison for Black people who were subjected to neglect, abuse, and oppression. There was a period between 1776 and 1865 when white people had a sense of superiority. A superiority complex to other races is a frustrating reality from which no one can escape. For close to a century, Black people remained enslaved, relying on the crumbs their masters extended to them. And in this shameful behavior, almost the entire world participated.

One Black woman who continues to impress and motivate the young generation is Mae Jemison—the first Black woman to go to space. She developed an interest in science from a very young age and was determined to reach for the stars. Jemison always wanted to be an astronaut and was disappointed to find that there were no female astronauts at that time.

What helped her not to stray away from her dream was Nichelle Nichols, who played the role of a lieutenant on a popular TV show, Star Trek. And this representation of women in space helped Jemison hold on to her dream of going to space.

The Destiny of Black Women in America

But this journey from the Earth to space had its set of challenges. Jemison was the only Black student in her class, which exposed her to racial discrimination. But she didn't let the systemic injustices stand between her and her dreams. And in 1987, she was among the 15 people chosen by NASA to go to space; there were around 2,000 applicants.

And from there began Jemison's rewarding career. She is now working on a project that ensures the journey of humans to another star in the next 100 years. Her contributions to science have paved the way for young girls who once used to be hesitant to pursue science; she will forever be their Nichelle Nichols.

Mae Jemison's career does ring a bell—many young Black women can share their stories of being discriminated against at their schools or colleges. Racism doesn't go away; it's not a switch that can be turned off. Yes, it's a harsh reality of today's world—in fact, it has been a constant feature in every century.

But there are two options for people: surrender or keep fighting. Surrendering is easy; you have to make zero effort and be happy with whatever you get, but through fighting, you can do the impossible. For so many people, Mae Jemison's desire to go to space would have been preposterous—the wishful thinking of a child. But through her hard work, she showed the world that one can achieve anything through grit and determination.

9.3 Embracing Empowerment and Equality for All

The civil rights movement played a crucial role in allowing the Black community in America to fight against the discrimination they faced. But it also had other roles to play, holding corporations accountable for not embracing America's diversity. Do you know there was a time when Black workers weren't allowed to use the white-only washrooms in their offices? They had to find a washroom for themselves in the office building during their working hours. The change was inevitable.

And why did corporates have to accept diversity? It was essential because they had to make a loud statement that they acknowledged that their target market was not only white. For how many years did we look at TV and magazines and find zero Black representation?

Imagine this: a nine-year-old Black child desperately waits for her Christmas gift. On the morning of Christmas, she hurriedly goes to the living room where the tree is kept and looks for her gift. She finds a box that looks like one that comes with a doll.

As she opens it, she finds a doll that looks nothing like her. And although she loves it, she doesn't find it relatable. Why can't a doll be like her? Why can't her hair be like hers? These questions do dominate young girls' minds, and they start feeling excluded.

And it wasn't about one product. White children were featured in ads for amusement parks, toys, snacks, and other kids-related products. It felt as if Black people did not exist—as if they were not sitting at the kitchen counter asking their parents to buy ice cream on a hot summer's day, or that they didn't want to go to Disneyland during their school vacations.

It was in 1967 that Mattel—the company responsible for manufacturing the world's most popular doll, 'Barbie'—launched a colored Barbie 'Francie'. But since the features of this doll were not close to that of a Black woman, the doll wasn't classified as a Black Barbie doll. In 1978, Kitty Black Perkins designed the first-ever Black Barbie for Mattel. The doll debuted in 1979, almost two decades after the launch of the original Barbie.

But this debut had (and still holds) a lot of importance. It was important for the Black community to ensure that their representation matters. The fight to get the first Black Barbie out in the world may seem a little insignificant, but it was important for the inclusion of the Black community in the mainstream.

And the same principles are held for politics, education, and entertainment. Today, we see Vice President Kamala Harris dominating U.S. politics. And as she appears on TV, young Black women and girls will imagine a time where they will be standing where Kamala Harris is standing today. Such representation goes a long way in aspiring girls and women, motivating them to keep fighting for their dreams and not settle for less.

Depression and losing the will to shoot for the stars have a way of creeping in suddenly. There are times when you may think that everything is against you, and that there is no way for you to reach the goal you have set for yourself. But things can be moved—the obstacles lying on your road to success can be removed, and you can have the road to yourself.

What you need in circumstances when everything seems lost—when you lose hope to keep trying—is a constant reminder that there were women who fought against all odds and refused to compromise or accept their fate. These women were deprived of all the luxuries in the world, and yet they fought so that you could get up and chase your dreams.

Celebrating Excellence

Kamala Harris' remarkable ascension to power might not have been possible, had political activist Shirley Chisholm not tried to become a forceful political figure in the country. In 1968, she became the first Black woman in Congress, and in 1972, she was the first Black woman to seek the nomination for President of the United States.

She once said: "You don't make progress by standing on the sidelines, whimpering, and complaining. You make progress by implementing ideas." And this woman was born in the 1920s when segregation and discrimination were still rife, and yet she didn't let her circumstances decide what she could or couldn't do.

Her other quote should serve as a reminder for all young women who are not sure if they have it in them to keep working toward their goals. "We must reject not only the stereotypes that others have of us but also those that we have of ourselves," says Shirly Chisholm. And this is so true. Black Excellence is your Destiny.

For years, the Black community allowed others to do their bidding. The powerful people sitting in high offices made policies that didn't consider the challenges Black people faced. For instance, while the end of the Civil War brought a victory for the Black population in terms of their right to vote, the situation on the ground was quite the opposite.

Most states introduced "criteria to qualify for voting" that included literacy tests that were long and confusing and seemed to be designed to flunk the candidate. But this criterion meant that Black people who were from low-income households and couldn't go to school because of their poverty had higher chances of failing the test and thus being deprived of the opportunity to cast their vote.

The Destiny of Black Women in America

The first legislation that was introduced to grant some respect to the Black community was the Civil Rights Act of 1957, which called for prosecution of anyone who willfully tried to prohibit anyone from voting.

This legislation was a small victory in what seemed a series of barriers that Black people had to pass to fight for their rights.

And from that time, we finally reached 2020, when Kamala Harris became the first Black woman vice president. But this victory doesn't mean that all is well in America and that the fight of Black women against a system that is inherently against them is over. Prominent writer Marianne Schnall, who works to amplify women's voices, published an article in Forbes, titled 'New Report on The State of Black Women in American Politics Highlights Both Progress and Untapped Potential'.

While the article mentioned Harris's success as a turning point for Black women, it also includes quotes from representatives from the Centre for American Women and Politics (CAWP) and the Higher Heights Leadership Fund (an organization working to build the collective power of Black women), who agree that there is still a tremendous opportunity for growth of Black women.

Over the years, and especially during the lead-up to elections, many Black women participated in political activities to make their voices heard. By doing so, they tell all young Black women and girls that they also have to participate in the political process if they wish to see the change and a shift from the status quo.

Throughout history, and not just in America, there have been instances when the Black community was oppressed, sometimes violently. But if history is any guide, Black people have always managed to break the shackles of oppression and occupation. They have emerged victorious and have not relied on anyone to fight for their freedom.

Black people have been criticized for their actions, but they remained steadfast. And now, they have come to a time—a moment that will forever be remembered in history—where Black women are some of the most powerful women in America.

And the report on the state of Black women in politics highlights the promising entry of more and more Black women into politics. In the 2020 presidential election, more than two-thirds of Black women voted, which is a victory for all of us. There are other great insights—a record number of Black women ran for congressional offices, and most of them won. Black women also reached a record high in state legislative representation in 2021. Black women also hold top posts in eight out of 100 most populous cities.

But while these statistics are heartwarming, they should not be enough for Black women to have a long way to go to have an influential presence in the American political landscape. For example, the report says, "Despite being 7.8 percent of the population, Black women are less than 5 percent of officeholders elected to statewide executive offices, Congress and state legislatures." It further adds, "Just 17 Black women have ever held statewide elected executive offices, and no Black woman has ever been elected governor."

The fact that a Black woman was the First Lady of the U.S. in 2008 and remained so for two terms and the fact that the current Vice President of the U.S. is a Black woman cannot wash away the stark reality—Black women are still underrepresented in politics. And it's on us—you and other young Black women to come forward and become a loud voice in politics. And why do these representations matter? They do so because they motivate countless other women to follow in their footsteps.

Conclusion

Reflecting on Black Women's Contributions

You may be overwhelmed to read about the successes of so many Black women. In the 21st century, it seems almost impossible to accept that the slavery period existed in American history. But in a way, this surprise highlights how far we've come. It shows that all the ills of society can be defeated, and that time is the best healer of the wounds of the past.

In this enthusiasm, we should not forget that the struggles and challenges for so many Black women are still there. What's different this time is that many Black women are now coming forward to tell their stories in hopes that other young women will derive inspiration from their struggle and the path they chose for themselves.

From top-rated actors and successful TV producers to well-respected astronauts, Black women have told the world that they're capable of achieving the stars. It is so emotional for so many people to witness the remarkable rise of Black women.

The past does have the habit of showing its glimpses of every now and then, and yes, it hurts to know what our forefathers may have gone through. But life also asks us to move on. We can channel the feelings of anger and disappointment toward something good. It's not advisable to let the anger consume us.

This book has one purpose: to tell readers how Black women managed to fight against the bad times and how they made a name for themselves. We have examples of so many Black men who are respected for their fight against racism and discrimination, and who are towering personalities in their fields.

It is, however, equally important to acknowledge and pay respect to the tireless efforts of Black women who fought together with Black men and ensured that their community's voice is respected and honored.

Black men's journey toward liberation and freedom wouldn't have been possible had they not had the support of remarkable Black women who had nerves of steel and who didn't think twice before helping their people. We must acknowledge that both men and women abolitionists played their role in the fight for freedom, which has now brought us to a point where we can live freely, chasing our dreams and raising our families.

Also, in a world marred by stereotypes against Black men, it is important to reiterate that most Black men are standing right beside Black women, helping them follow their dreams. They're there to support women and help them remove the roadblocks laid out in their path to success.

When we look at what these dedicated people achieved with perhaps a quarter of resources as compared to what we have now, we can't help but wonder how great their strength could be. Today, we are living in the golden age of development, and it is now on us to make the most of it.

Looking Towards a Brighter Future

I wish that everyone who has come this far will make a pledge not to let their intrusive thoughts get the better of them. I want them to tell themselves over and over that they're destined for great things and that they will work hard to achieve their dreams.

Once you've finished this book, I want you to scream with all your might and say, "I CAN!" Yes, you can! Like all those women who came before you, you can turn your life around and make the impossible possible. You can break the shackles of negativity and let people know that you are the next big thing.

Once you start chasing your dreams, you'll soon see your name in the list of high achievers, and once you achieve that, you won't make only yourself proud but also the countless young Black women who may be looking for an inspiration to follow their dreams.

The history and achievements of Black women are so rich that you'll feel a twinge of guilt for ever doubting your capabilities. Racism and discrimination are scourge of society, but we now have tools to fight against such inequality.

In your journey toward excellence, you'll never find yourself alone! This book will keep reminding you that you have the blessings of so many great women who will forever be your guiding light!

"Celebrating Excellence: The Destiny of Black Women in Americas"

Tolbert Morris Jr

About Author

Tolbert Morris is a retired Navy Veteran having served 20 honorable years in the U.S. Navy. In his continued service to the community, Mr. Morris and his wife, Janice T., Morris, the CEO and COO of Helping Hands Outreach (HHO), have been dedicated to bridging the digital divide since establishing the organization in 2001. In 2004, he and his wife Janice expanded the services of the HHO by opening the Helping Hands Health Clinic, aiming to address the shortage of healthcare for uninsured and underinsured citizens in Rockdale County and the Metro Atlanta area.

Tolbert's passion for education and empowering the next generation is truly inspiring. His influential role as a member of the Rockdale County School Board of Education from 2004 to 2008 enabled him to play a crucial role in establishing the Rockdale Career Academy, opening doors for students to develop practical skills for their future careers.

Moreover, he initiated a summer school program for at-risk students. Through these efforts, he has exemplified his passion for uplifting the next generation and equipping them with the tools they need to succeed.